Touching
A Dead Man

dl foster

D1302485

Touching A Dead Man

One man's explosive story of
deliverance from homosexuality

dl foster

Unless otherwise noted, scripture quotations are taken from the King James Version of the Bible. Public domain. Scripture quotations marked NIV taken from the Holy Bible, New International Version® Copyright 1973,1978,1984 by International Bible Society. Used by permission.

Additional copies of this book may be obtained by writing to:
DL Foster
Post Office Box 960387
Riverdale, Georgia 30296-0387
Or via email at TouchingDeadMan@aol.com

TOUCHING A DEAD MAN
Copyright © 2002 by Darryl L. Foster
First printing • 300 copies • September 2002
ISBN 0-9723510-0-0
Library of Congress Control Number: 2002094669

Printed in the United States of America
Morris Publishing
3212 East Hwy 30
Kearney, NE 68847
800-650-7888
www.morrispublishing.com

Cover design by the author. All rights reserved.

Contents

Foreword

This book is not for 'spiritual wimps' nor 'scary cats in the Kingdom'. "Touching a Dead Man" is for those that are willing to *come out the closet, shut the door – but not be afraid to return to snatch another brother or sister out of the trap of lust!*

The author is bold, brave and committed to help as many in the body of Christ that satan as well as some churches, have written off.

If you're ready for a challenge...read this book. If you're ready to hear bare facts of truth...read this book. If you are wondering if deliverance and victory is available to you, read this book. You will be informed, you will at times be alarmed, you will be shocked and you will be challenged to ask God what you can do to prevent another man or woman's death in sin.

I salute this wonderful man of God that has made a choice to believe that we are made in the image and likeness of God. That every man, woman, boy and girl has a right to salvation, victory and deliverance. That Jesus Christ was 'hung up for our hang ups' therefore we can get up out of our mess! In fact, our **mess can become our message! Preach, Pastor Preach!** Your life testimony has promoted you to the status of "Living Epistle".

-Dr. Wanda A. Turner
CEO, MECCA Ministries, Intl
Author: *Sex Traps, Even with my Issues, I stood in the Flames*

A Word of Prophecy

June 22, 1996, Waco, Texas

I am looking at several books that are coming out of your hands. I heard the word this morning, but I didn't see you today. I don't know if you are visiting or a member, I'm not in the Spirit on that, but I am in the Spirit on this. I see several books that are coming out of your hands. And the books are going to bring you a national notoriety. God is raising you for an hour such as this. And in the midst of God raising you, God is going to cause the skeptic that said 6 years ago that you could not have gotten to the place that you are right now... but because God is God all by himself... God is going to do it, and speed up your miracle."

Prophet Aubrey Shines, Glory to Glory Ministries

"Believe in the Lord your God, shall ye be established, believe in his prophets, so shall ye prosper."
2 Chronicles 20:20

"For as the rain cometh down, and the snow from heaven and returneth not thither, but watereth the earth, and maketh it bring forth and bud, that it may give seed to the sower, and bread to the eater: So shall my word be that goeth forth out of my mouth, it shall not return unto me void, but it shall accomplish that which I please, and it shall prosper in the thing whereunto I sent it."
Isaiah 55:10,11

Acknowledgements & Thanks

First praises and glory to the Father, Son and Holy Ghost. My deepest gratitude to the following:

To my mother, father, sisters and brothers: thanks for loving your brother who was dead, but now lives.

To my wife Dee and my children: thank you from the bottom of my heart for enduring to see my vision become a reality. Thank you for believing in me and pushing me to do God's will.

To the members of Restoration Sanctuary International Church: it's a great joy to serve you and lead you into the greatness God has purposed for us.

To Dr. Gilbert and Gail Gillum, Jr., Pastor (Drs) Charles and Gloria Rodgers, Pastor Martin and Evangelist Marissa Johnson, for your work in shaping me. Your labor and patience was not in vain.

To Valerie Lowe of *Charisma*. Thanks for your courage and faith in God to write "Let's stop hiding from the pain."

To Dr. Frederick K.C. Price: Inspiration is a powerful thing!

To my ministry partners and friends Evangelist Miriam Pass-more and Minister Chris Johnson, Sr. for encouraging me.

To Pastors around the country who are not just noticing the need, but taking action.

To COGIC: thank you for the good and the bad.

To each and every person who has shared your burdens, your testimony, your prayers and encouragement with me.

Additionally, I want to thank the production staff at Morris Publishing for the excellent help in producing this book.

A prayer

Father God, I bless you and praise you for revealing your heart and desire that all men would experience salvation through Jesus Christ. I thank you for the unimpeachable love you have shown to me and my seed. By giving me this vision to write *Touching a Dead Man*, you have destroyed the power of secrecy and the yoke of bondage for so many people. Let this work, I pray Lord, be tried in fire and stand not because of me, but because of you.

Let your love, truth, mercy, goodness, grace, and tenderness speak from the pages. Let your righteousness and judgment stand watch in the wings. Let the words that I write and the meditations of my heart be acceptable in thy sight. Give life to the lifeless and hope to the hopeless. This is my prayer and my desire to you.

Completely, in the name of the Lord Jesus, Amen.

Dedications

Lovingly dedicated to

To my wife Dee. I owe all of this to you and your precious,
patient love.

To my friends in ministry. Write your vision and make it plain.

To all of my friends whom I met while "in the life".
You too, can be free.

INTRODUCTION
Just to share with you

I want to thank you for opening up the pages of this book. By writing it I took a chance. I know that you have the power to reject me and what I say or you have the same power to embrace me and what I say. I hope that you will choose to embrace, not out of sympathy, but because you believe what I am attempting to share is truth and freedom.

In this book are the window panes of my life. I wrote it because I'm no longer ashamed or afraid of people knowing what God did for me. These panes, cleaned thoroughly by the blood of Jesus, are an invitation to look in. As you do, feel free to laugh with me, to rejoice with me. You can cry with me or be sad and disturbed at the things, which have befallen me and others mentioned in this story.

Ultimately, when all of the looking is over, when you have finished the last word on the last page, when your emotions are spent and your belief system challenged, my deepest desire is for the Lord Jesus Christ to be glorified. It's only because of Him that I live, move and have my being.

I know that some may think that I have said what I have said in order to gain some sort of contrived notoriety, but the truth of the matter is that I am only a small fish in a big pond trying to make a little ripple. *Touching A Dead Man* wasn't written as a gossip item or name-dropping gimmick. However, reality is reality and part of the problem in dealing with homosexuality is the timorous approach, if at all, of church leadership. Therefore, it became clear to me that while I was obligated to be as frank and respectful as possible, the project was meant to knock the devil off his perch.

I don't expect everyone to understand or support this book. I expect to be criticized possibly even maligned. But it's a small price to pay to help someone understand that they don't have to live beneath their privilege and right to freedom as a child of God. I never set out to hear the disturbing stories of abuse suffered at the hands of the church, nor did I run with wild abandon to discover the disgusting secrets hidden behind closed doors. It is a terrible place to be in where God chooses you to make known that which is undesirable.

People normally use the saying "we are God's eyes, ears and hands" to emphasize that God uses people to accomplish His work. I agree with that, but have we forgotten that the "eyes of the Lord are in every place beholding the good and the evil" (Proverbs 15:3)? If that is true, then God will also use certain of His servants to behold and expose the evil, even if it is within His house.

He used Ezekiel for such a purpose. It is no spot of glory for the man or woman being used, because the usual reaction is one of rejection. `

> *And he [the Lord God] brought me to the*
> *door of the court; and when I looked, behold*
> *a hole in the wall.*
> *Then he said to me, Son of man, dig*
> *now in the wall: and when I had digged in*

2

the wall, behold a door. And he said unto
me, Go in, and behold the wicked
abominations that they do here.
So I went in and saw; and behold every form
of creeping things, and abominable beasts
and all the idols of the HOUSE OF
ISREAL (my caps), portrayed upon the wall
round about.
Then he said to me Hast thou seen this, O
son of man? Turn thee yet again and thou
shalt see great abominations than these.
And he brought me into the inner court of
the Lord's house and, behold at the door of
the temple of the Lord, between the porch
and the altar, were about five and twenty
men with their backs toward the temple of
the Lord, and their faces toward the east; and
they worshiped the sun toward the
east. (Ezekiel 8:7-10,15,16)

This incredible season of hidden sin and willful misconduct by both those in leadership and the people, proceeded an awful time. Their actions, which they assumed God did not see, were being recorded by heavenly eyes and shown to earthly eyes. Soon, Isreal forfeited the glory of the Lord. Is this what we want as we continue to carry on secret sins in the church and then display hostility and anger when God sends someone to call us out of it? I pray that this is not your desire. It's certainly not mine. I want to be saved and I want to obey God.

Touching a Dead Man was a winding evolution of sorts, starting as a testimony project on our outreach ministry (WITNESS!) website. But much of the supporting material is a culmination of years of personal observation, research, and experience. Several close friends begin urging me on more than one occasion to share my story with a larger audience. I listened to them and as I worked towards completion, it became apparent to me that it was much more than I had expected it to be.

As I wrote, the Holy Spirit told me to write and share completely. The good, the bad and the ugly, as well as the victory and joys, were to be laid out. It's been a long time since that clear night in March 1996 when I first received a command from the Lord to write this book. It has been an even longer time since He told me in April 1990 to "tell everyone what I did for you." But it's always a long road walking into purpose. We don't always immediately obey God when He speaks, but in the long run (or walk), obedience proves to be better than sacrifice.

I began receiving email after email from people all over the country, telling me how powerful and moving my story was. For the most part, it came from other men and women who, like me, had battled to overcome this unwanted part of our lives. Even as I took a step back and reread what I had written, I too was moved to tears and renewed praise to God for all that He had brought me through. Someone once said if you can think, then you can thank!

Somewhere in the between time, the Lord brought the words of the prophecy seeded into my life by Prophet Aubrey Shines to my remembrance (page v). Many people began asking me when my "book" was coming out. At first, I was flattered, but thought a book was light years in the future. But the Lord spoke to my heart and said "believe my prophets, and so shall ye prosper." Although a word of prophecy can be spoken or confirmed in your life, unless you are willing to become an active participant in it, it will not come to pass.

When I first learned Prophet Shines was coming to conduct revival at our church in Waco in June 1996, I was disappointed because I didn't believe in the so-called prophets in the church. I was convinced that the only message they could deliver involved "cars, husbands and houses." And frankly, I didn't want to hear anything he had to say. But, being obedient to my Pastor who requested that all ministers be present in support of the revival, I went.

June 1996 found me in the midst of one of the most difficult trials of faith I had ever experienced and to tell you the truth my faith in God and His promises were at an all time low. I felt like a zombie, just going through the motions of church. Lifting up my hands, but having them fall back down in defeat. Dancing with no joy in my heart. Singing unto the Lord, but not hearing the words come back to me. I doubted that God had called me into ministry, doubted that he had told me to write this book, doubted that He had told me to speak out and help others in homosexual lifestyle. My backsliding fuse was short and burning fast.

I recall how I mumbled and grumbled to my wife after church that Sunday and then that night, when the Prophet called me up, I was very scared because I thought God was going to chastise me in front of everyone, because I didn't believe. I can laugh now, but it wasn't at all funny then. Now, Lord, I do believe!

And so I prayed, recommitted myself to loving God with my whole heart, believed the word of prophecy and began to work on *Touching a Dead Man* - the book. What you will be reading contains a portion of the original manuscript I wrote in 1996. When I had completed that first draft after long nights of pecking and typing, God said to me "Put it on the shelf. You now have to live it." Yes, how can you teach when you have not lived what you seek to teach? I understand perfectly why He had me to do then what He wanted me to do now.

The title for the book came from an inspirational conversation I had several years ago with a precious friend of mine, Minister Charlotte Ann Moore of Dallas.

The physical act of writing about your life is, within itself, extremely liberating. Best selling author William Zinsser says it "creates a powerful mental search mechanism." Inexpressible events and circumstances that have long lay dormant, no matter how good or bad, are called forth from the power of the memory. Remembering empowers the storyteller in a way that nothing else can, simply because you tell the story. I'm glad God let me remember the hurt, the pain and the trauma I've endured. I'm glad I can recall how it used to be. The storm is over now. However, without the memory of the storm, the ensuing peace can, at best, be fragile and temporary. Without a recollection of the battle, the victory is somehow hollow, bittersweet and meaningless.

If you think that my story is unique, of course I'm grateful but it's really not. No one has ever come into this world and escaped trouble, so in that respect, I'm no different than you. However, what gives my life profound meaning is that I now believe and trust on the Lord Jesus. This new life of relationship with the man of my dreams has birthed an understanding that he will walk with me through every valley from now on.

Unlike the male lovers I had, this man, The Christ, will never leave me nor forsake me. On the other side of the dark days is a bright new beginning. I face each new day with the steadfast hope of overcoming. I have gained brand new mercy for a brand new day.

By truthfully sharing with you my story, *Touching a Dead Man*, I pray that you too, will see and convincingly know that no matter what you've done or how long you've done it, or who you've done it with, your life is never beyond repair. From a life of sexual brokenness, constant yearning, self devaluation and rebellion, God has carried me into a place of joy and fulfillment.

I've discovered that reality in Jesus Christ. That is the hope for all of us in this sometimes chaotic and unexplainable world.

Darryl L. Foster
2002, A.D.

PART ONE

Growing up and out in the black church:

the seeds of sickness

*"Now a man named Lazarus was sick. He was
from Bethany, the village of Mary and her sister
Martha. So the sisters sent word to Jesus, Lord, the
one you love is sick. When he heard this, Jesus said,
This sickness will not end in death. No, it is for
God's glory, so that God's son may be glorified
through it. Yet, when he heard that Lazarus was
sick, he stayed where he was for two more days."*
The Gospel according to St. John,
Chapter 11, verses 1,2,4,6 (NIV)

1
Roots, running deep

I was born into a "church family." In our brand of African American religious tradition, the generations of family who served in the church were worn like a badge of honor. Church was the one place where, in spite of the hardships of outside pressures, especially racism, blacks could feel equal, special and respected. Black people knew the church had sustained them, given them faith in God and themselves to overcome the crush of being different in other's eyes. This was the world, caught in the crosshairs of race, religion and sexuality, good and bad, which I inherited.

My grandpa, Ezekiel Foster, was a model Church of God in Christ (COGIC) Pentecostal preacher. He and his wife Pearl were holiness pioneers who raised their 13 children in the strictest way possible: strong, yet fiercely devoted to their well being. Their six acre family farm was situated on the rural subdivision known as "Tomlinson Hill." Tomlinson Hill sat midway between the small

9

Central Texas towns of Marlin and Lott. The farm served as the backdrop for Ezekiel and Pearl's belief that children should work and support the family.

For most rural black Texas families, long days and even longer hours in the cotton fields were a fact of daily life. Consequently, my mother, called Mae by her brothers and sisters, only completed 8th grade schooling since she was required to be in the fields most of the time. The last time she saw the inside of a school was in 1949 at age 17.

My grandmother ~affectionately known as Big Mama~ died mysteriously in 1965. I was at the tender age of 4. My grandpa's parents, Gus and Annie, we were told, came to Texas from Alabama, but they were not of the holiness faith. That part of my legacy began with my grandpa getting saved and then being called to preach in early 1930's.

Though I didn't know my grandpa well until his later years, I loved him with all my heart. I was drawn to his quiet strength. I remember his raspy preaching voice calling my mother's name as he left from visits in his old '64 Chevrolet pickup truck. He'd bought that truck the year before Big Mama died and drove it until he also died. We hitched bumper rides on it when he wasn't looking.

"Mae," he'd say, "I'll be back to check on you baby."

After Big Mama died, he continued to come and visit mother, maybe because she had a large family and no husband. Whenever Grandpa showed up, we rushed out to meet him. He didn't have to give us a dime, we were just glad to see him. As an extra treat, he usually brought us large tubs of his famous pears and peaches from his farm. After all, we were children without a father and his care for us meant the whole wide world.

10

My Grandpa was a man full of conviction. He founded a COGIC in a small Texas town. It was said that his preaching was so powerful, that the rafters of the church vibrated. His sermon notes, found years after he died, revealed a man intensely concerned about current events and the way the church should interpret them. He always incorporated this into his messages. Mother told us people said he preached as if he had a theology degree, but in reality, he'd never been past what was a 3rd grade education.

I'm sure that the pressure to be a man of dignity, while facing the callous attacks of racism, forged him into a man who knew what he had to do. As a matter of fact he and Pearl knew that they were obligated to raise strong, God-fearing children who would have a better life than they had. (They lost only one child, their beautiful, 13-year-old daughter Idella. She was struck by lightening on the family's first day at their new Tomlinson Hill homestead.)

My Grandpa's dream is the dream of every father. I look at my children and hope for them the same thing my grandfather hoped for his children. I want them to learn how to be strong and to love God with all their heart. Grandpa gave me that legacy. Be strong and love God with all your heart.

When he came to his declining years and his health began to fail, he never complained about his pains. During the final days of his life, until he went home to be with the Lord, mother would stand silently by his bedside, just looking at him with love and respect. I know that for her, she had come full circle. She had ended a rebellious period in her life and I sensed that she was glad that her daddy raised her to turn and trust God. Once she whispered reverently to me, "Daddy never complains."

My father, Clifton, was a preacher too, but with him, it was a different story. Mother says the day I was born in a little house right off Independence Street in Cameron, Texas, he wasn't around. Like a jack in the box, he popped in and out of my life, without me realizing who he was. In 1969, we moved to the small central Texas community of Marlin to be a little closer to my Grandpa.

Shortly thereafter, at age 7, I met my father for the first time, though I was too young to understand who he was. He gave my little brother and me a few dollars, patted us on the head and left. Six years later I saw him again. This time I was full with years of anger, hostility and hatred at his uncaring abandonment. Because my daddy was a preacher, we had several brushes with him at church meetings. It was always the same.

"Do we call him daddy?" my little brother asked me one time. He looked at me, wide-eyed and innocent, hoping his big brother had the right answer. After thinking about it, I said, "No, we'll just call him sir." I was determined to be as cold as possible. We saw him at the church meeting (he was pastoring at the time), but he was devoid of any emotional offering to us.

My daddy mechanically rubbed our heads and offered us a few dollars apiece. This time I refused. I hated him so much I couldn't have cared if it was a thousand dollars. It couldn't bring back all the years he left us to struggle alone. It couldn't answer all the unanswered questions. After that encounter, I did not see him again until I was well into adulthood.

Mother had to work two jobs back to back to support us. Even with that, we were forced to accept welfare, which never seemed to be enough. I watched her come in from one job at the nursing home, tired and beaten from the long walk, just long enough to give instructions, check on us and then be off to her second job as a short order cook at a hotel. She never abandoned us, but struggled hard with the burden of having to leave us alone. The money was always short or missing in action.

There were many times, because we didn't have the money, utilities were abruptly shut off, the water, the electric and gas. Some-times it happened in the dead of winter.

We learned to live with fear and rats. Neither of which was going away. One night, we were all sitting in the living room joking about different things. My sister Myra and her two kids had come up from where she lived near Houston and so our house was full. Suddenly, out of nowhere a huge rat jetted into the room and darted around crazily, eventually running right under our feet! I can only compare it to being on a plane about to crash. We dived, screamed, jumped, and ran, falling over each other in total fright! Myra and I ended up standing on the couch clinging to each other for dear life! For years, I had nightmares about rats, and to this day I am still deathly afraid of all things rodent. No, the Lord hasn't delivered me from that yet!

Yet, those times also held some of the most beautiful memories of my childhood. Our family seemed so close and loving when we faced hard times together. We were amazingly resourceful and helpful to each other. It's true, love is tried and proven in adversity.

Mother was an excellent seamstress and sewed together pieces of old clothes and quilts to keep us extra warm. She always had candles ready to light at night after she had no money to pay the light bill but knew we had to be at school the next day. When food was scarce, we ate our syrup sandwiches for lunch and our peanut butter sandwiches for dinner. For dessert, we had a delicious sugar sandwich.

We'd cackle and hee-haw all night long about the crazy things only we Foster children could laugh about. Who would have believed that once a huge rat ate part of the leftover fried chicken? We alternately joked and griped about who would clean and lime the outhouse next. Yes, I did say outhouse. The eight of us hung with our mother, the queen of our life. And like her father, she endured it all without complaint.

My oldest brother, Charles, was more like a father to us. As the oldest, he had to take that role. When Mother was away at work, he was the one who disciplined us, told us when to come home, when to go to bed and the one who cooked for us. He later became a Pentagon chef in his 22 year military career. As long as I could remember, my oldest sister Myra had lived away from home. My second oldest brother Lance stayed in trouble; he was the black militant in the family. He couldn't stand "the man" or his rules. That left in order Robert, me, Dwight, Tracy and my baby sister Tammy.

Reading and writing were always my passion. Reading was an escape for me from the "boy" things I couldn't do. My mother had purchased a set of World Book encyclopedia's in 1963 and I read each one of them over and over. I was fascinated at all the foreign places like Peking, Paris and Moscow where the world seemed to be so drastically different from small town Marlin. History and geography were always my favorite subjects. My mother still has that same set, although most of the volumes are pretty worn.

I know that we all loved each other, but in our house, the words *I love you* were seldom heard or spoken. We were not an affectionate family: we didn't hug and kiss each other at all. Now, that I'm a father, I hug and kiss my children a lot. I tell them I love them and ask them if they love me. If they fuss and fight, I require them to hug and kiss as part of their forgiving process. Articulating those words and actions in the family has become very important to me.

Also, like most parents who were of the postwar generation my mother came from, talking about sexual issues was something that simply did not happen. I never heard my mother talk about things related to sex. She may have been uncomfortable with it or just kept quiet as her parents before had. Years later as I thought about it, I asked myself, "What could she have told me?"

Talking about sex and sexuality with their children is a difficult thing for most parents. You just think that your kids will always be the sweet, innocent little tykes you may not have wanted to grow up so fast. But now, reality and necessity dictate that parents shed the coyness about sex and sexual things and make it a priority for their kids from a biblical perspective. That perspective rotates around the traditional family.   As a young boy I had plenty questions. I could never understand why my father wasn't there to help us.

When other kids at school talked about their dads, I slipped away, hurt and ashamed because I didn't know if my own father loved me or if he even knew I was alive. I missed his touch and his voice. Though I never had it, it was just one of those things I knew was missing from my life. To this day, I don't know why I was born illegitimate to two people ~a preacher and a preacher's daughter~ who should have known better. But such is life. My mother was very guarded about her personal life and only vaguely explained why she and my father weren't together. One thing she didn't do, she chose not to criticize or denigrate him before us.

I always dreaded seeing my reflection in the mirror. When I did force myself to look, a weak, timid boy, full of fear, self-loathing and pain stared back. I couldn't relate to other boys my age except in one way. And that was a deep, dark secret I hoped no one would ever discover. A secret that was too big for a small heart like mine to

15

contain. It was my mark of shame, like Cain, a burden I was forced to buckle under for much of my life. I said before my mother was the queen of my life, but a woman can't teach a boy to be a man.

The void left by my Father's absence exacerbated my sense of alienation. Out of five boys in my family, I considered myself the "weakest link." I was the first one to cry, always being teased and called sissy, always emotional and sensitive. In the absence of my father, I developed a deep longing for a man to hold me in his arms, tell me he loved me and that I was valuable to him. It was a constant craving that slowly defined who I was to become. It was like standing on the shore of a sea you could never sail across. I needed a man's touch and healthy affirmation.

Instead of receiving the affirmation of other males, the gaps between us widened. I didn't fit into their plans or games. I was never called to be part of the "team." It was an unspoken rule that I was not "one of them." The rejection of this basic, but important social connection affected my mental health, which in turn soon effected my physical reactions.

I hate that commercial by Gatorade. "Is it in you?" they ask. It's a subliminal taunt to all of us nonathletic types. I don't think I have any of "it" running through my veins, let alone seeping out when I get hot. Growing up, the thought of football, baseball and basketball and other contact sports frightened me. I accepted that I couldn't do it, simply because they said I couldn't. Other boys told me that since I was a sissy, these games were not the games that sissies could play. Without the benefit of a father or male friends, I never seemed to understood why sports was so important.

I grew up in a neighborhood of dirt streets, outhouses, and wood stoves. It was a place where life and death eyed each other like the

Hatfields and the McCoys. Folks around the 'hood had crazy nicknames like "Caveman", "Biggie Rat", "Foots" and "Lee-Lee". Hardly any of us knew each other's real names.

The neighborhood was made up mainly of Blacks and Hispanics. In May we celebrated Cinco de Mayo. Then in June, we headed down to the old Baptist Tabernacle at the far end of Commerce Street to enjoy the soul food and *very* soulful people during Juneteenth.

One of our neighbors, old Mr. Perry Reed, lived across the street from us. He was a recluse, living in his own little world until one day we all began smelling something so rancid; it made you want to puke. That's when the police discovered him in his house as dead as the fake dime store flowers he had in his yard. He had set himself on fire.

Behind us lived Mr. Lolo (pronounced low-low). Mr. Lolo was, like most of the Hispanics in the neighborhood, short, almost a midget. But also some of the nicest folks you'd ever want to meet. He was known throughout the community (especially by us kids) for the peach trees growing in his garden. The fruit from those trees were the largest, juiciest and sweetest I have ever seen. They were the source of constant temptation. Many times we simply could not resist. My brothers and I formed the "Peach Patrol" and conducted late night peach raids.

Next to us, across the cornfield lived sweet old Mrs. Humphrey. She owned a cute little house dog which met an unfortunate fate. The poor pooch decided to escape Mrs. Humphrey's protective environment to explore the outside world once.

It was a fatal mistake. Several stray dogs and our dog, "Mean", dispatched the poor little thing to dog heaven in a bad fight.

Down the street, lived Ms Purdue (pronounced purr-doo) and all of her kids. They were hard, rowdy and a serious mistake to cross in a

17

fight. And that was just the girls! Typically, when one member of the family got into a fight, you could expect that everyone else was going to get a lick or two in also.

Directly across the street was the Davila family. They were probably the most "well to do" in the neighborhood. By that I mean the Davila's had a nice car and a nice house with nice green grass that they watered every day. They were Pentecostals like us, but they went to the Spanish Assembly of God. Life was vibrant on our street, but for me, not necessarily good.

All the guys it seemed, were super athletes. They went after it with gusto, but I was afraid of being hit too hard and crying. I was scared that I would touch another boy and he would somehow think that I was trying to feel him up. Yes, that nightmare came true. On a crowded school bus, I accidentally brushed up against a football "star" who yelled out "you faggot, don't touch me!" So, I shrank away from sports altogether. I was terrified of sports. It didn't help my image much, because all my brothers were into sports.

One sunny Saturday afternoon, when I was about 12, I found out just how "different" I was from other boys. Everybody gathered in front of the Brigette Toleston's house at the end of Brown Street. Regardless of the game of the day —football, baseball or some hoops— the end of Brown Street, in front of the Toleston's house was the field or the court. That day, from somewhere, an overwhelming urge gripped me. I wanted to play ball so bad. I guess the loneliness had gotten to be unbearable. I often played with the girls, but I longed to be with the guys. I didn't exactly know how to play ball but I knew I wanted to. I thought that if I could just convince them with my willingness and eagerness, they would accept me. Through their eyes, I began seeing sports as a way to feel and live out the "normal" carelessness like any other boy would.

Everyone jumped and yelled, jockeying for the best team lineup. I was left out, standing on the sidelines looking dejected, but nonetheless hopeful. As I watched, my young eyes soaked up the joy of their camaraderie. I listened to their callous joking and macho bragging. I wanted to be a part of their world. *Yes, this was something I wanted to do.* But I might as well had been invisible.

Finally, in desperation, I yelled out, "I want to play!" The response and the rejection was swift. "No, you sissy, only men can play this game!" another boy shot back at me. Hot, angry tears welled up in my eyes. *No, I don't want them to see me cry,* but I couldn't stop it. I knew I was losing, but maybe they would take pity on me.

"Can I just try?" I begged. I was heartsick with the isolation. Then, my own brother's voice shot out like a missile, "We don't want no girls playing with us," he fired off, "why don't you go home and play with the other girls?" At this, they all laughed. It was a direct hit. I didn't have to guess about it anymore; it was time to retreat. I was convinced after that incident that I would never be like them. *I wasn't a girl. Or was I?*

Charles left home in 1974 to join the Army. My brother Lance left when he was about 16, due to frequent "skirmishes" with Mother. He too, found his way into military service. Several years later, Robert struck out too and left, the third military man in the family. That left me as the oldest at home. The oldest, but the least qualified to be any type of role model to my remaining younger siblings.

19

The power of preaching in our churches is what has shaped the passion of our worship. Preaching was always seen as the "main course" of the Sunday gospel feast.

2

Sanctified Sanctimony

I remember that my mother was a powerful singer who was in big demand in the churches where we fellowshipped. Mother sang with the conviction of a woman who had been through some things in life. Her commanding voice was strong and deep, so she never used a microphone. She belted out old gospel classics like "I don't know what I would do (without the Lord)", one of her favorites. When she opened her mouth and testified with a song like "I'm a sol-jah!", folks would jump to their feet and respond "in the army of the Lord!" Her testimony songs always got the church to shouting and dancing. She got very irritated if people "drug" the song, as she called it because she felt the praise service should always be lively and full of joy.

My favorite picture of my mother is one of her when she was about 19. She took it while she was out in West Texas picking cotton with some of the other members of her family. If there was any such thing as a confident black "sista" back in those days, she definitely had that going on. Her pearly white teeth and full smile was set against a canvas of smooth black skin. She had her wavy hunk of coal black hair piled on her head in the graceful pompadour style of the day. She wore a beautiful white blouse which was set off with a pair of globed, bobbing, faux pearl earrings.

Salvation changed all that. Her childhood teachings said that holy women didn't wear the trappings of a Jezebelian culture, so she promptly threw all the makeup, jewelry, and flashy clothes away. Lately, my sister Tracy and I have convinced her to at least wear a nice church hat and some earrings. Mother always sent us to church when she couldn't go. Although I missed her presence, I was ok with that because I loved going to church. Church ferried me to the crossroads of sexuality.

I was not aware of my tendency to sexualize relationships with other males until I was about 11. The concept wasn't something I could identify with because I didn't realize the depth of the words "sissy" and "faggot". I knew by other's reactions, *something was different about me*, but just what that "difference" was I didn't know. It dawned on me one day in the sixth grade when I was at school chasing a white male friend on the playground. It was just normal kid's play, but when I caught him, a certain feeling (which I can't really explain) went through me as I held him.

Attending church does not save you, but going to a "holiness/ Pentecostal" church from infancy, certainly has the tendency to make you think you are saved. I believed I "got saved" also when I was 11. However, by the time I was 13, it was the homosexual thoughts, not my salvation that grew stronger. I first learned about homosexuality in my church youth classes.

21

The news from the Bible and my female teacher was stark and devastating to me when I first heard it. Homosexuals were hated and despicable creatures who were destined for hell. About six of us were a part of the youth group, Purity Class. The COGIC Purity Class was established in the early days of the church to keep youth pure and separated from the ways of the world, especially sex.

I still struggled against the emotions, thoughts and developing actions seeking to find a resting place within me. I seesawed between what my mind told me was wrong and what my body demanded to feel. It was tough for me not to fantasize about what it would feel like if a man touched me. I just knew it would feel wonderful and comforting to have someone want me, even if it were wrong.

At times, the curiosity of sexual exploration overwhelmed me and a deluge of unanswered questions cast an oppressive shadow over my troubled mind. What did a man really look like unclothed? What would I do if someone invited me to be with him? Would I feel love and pleasure like I had seen with heterosexual couples on television? Would he find me attractive? Acting out was out of the question. I did not want to die doing something wrong. If I did, I would find myself the permanent prisoner of devils. I definitely didn't want to go there. But eventually, even that fear wasn't enough to stem the assault on my God given sexual nature.

Growing up Pentecostal is one of the best things that can ever happen to a kid. With the kind of church we have, there's no need for movies, football games or parties to satisfy a person's need for excitement! I mean, they didn't call us "holy rollers" for nothing! With a Hammond B3 and Leslie speaker, a good drum set, a couple of solid tambourines and a nice thumping church floor, church could provide enough spills and thrills to last a lifetime. The preaching was always the main attraction. The power of preaching in our churches is what has shaped the passion of our worship. Preaching was always seen as the "main course" of the Sunday gospel feast.

William B. McClain writes in the *Leadership Handbook of Preaching and Worship*, "In the African American church, Sunday morning in Savannah is just like Sunday morning in Atlanta or New York or New Orleans or Oakland. It's Sunday and that's the time to *have church!*"[1]

We Black folk take our Sunday worship and preaching seriously! In our night services, it was nothing for us to shout and dance well past midnight. It's all about the joy of the Lord! Like a million other young wanna be saints, I learned how to "have church". At home, we learned to mimic the shouting sisters and beat our mother's cake pans for tambourines. Me and my brothers and sisters "shouted" until we sweated. Invariably in our home "play church" the sermon would always end on a "shouting note" (SAY YES!)

Amid the shouting, dancing and jubilance so fundamental to our worship experience, I pretended everything was okay. If we had "testimony service," I got up and gave my manufactured church testimony. It went something like this: "I thank the Lord for being here. Thank the Lord for my life, health and strength. Thank the Lord for being saved, sanctified and filled with the Holy Ghost. Want the saints to pray my strength in the Lord." That's what I said. Come on now; don't tell me you didn't say that at least once growing up!

I wasn't about to confess what was really swirling around in my head. I wasn't about to say that sometimes I wanted to touch other men. That would have gained me instant demon-possessed status. But that was reality and I knew the saints didn't want to hear about my realities, just the goodness of God.

23

I fasted on the traditional Tuesday and Friday COGIC corporate fast days. I went to church every time the doors were open and then some. I sang in the choir and stayed at all night tarry services, the "shut-ins". I wanted that devil and all of his sexual demons out of my life and I tried everything I knew to run him away for good.

It had been quite a while since I had a "girlfriend" so I decided to attempt a resurrection of my dormant heterosexual feelings. I was sure a girlfriend would chase away my homosexual thoughts and feelings. I picked out a beautiful girl from another city whose father was an elder in our district. We talked several times and I began telling other kids we were dating. It all fell apart when she summarily broke the news one night (over one of those exorbitant $2.00 church chili dogs) that she didn't "like" me. In the kind of church I grew up in, dating was sharply discouraged between males and females. We were always taught it would lead to fornication.

Far too many struggling
saints, whom I believe
receive deliverance,
become mired in
discouragement and get
out of the race, some
never to return.

3

Deliverance: Swept, Sealed *and* Garnished

*T*he front cover of the book *Exposing Spiritual Witchcraft*, depicted a huge spider spinning a sinister-looking web. The author, Apostle Jonas Clark of Florida was described as "anointed" and carrying a "refreshing voice of the Spirit." He wanted to educate believers on the dangers of spiritual witchcraft.

While reading the book's interesting claims, I came across a couple of paragraphs that threw me for a loop. They seemed like a couple of rotten apples hidden in a barrel of perfect fruit.

"I was preaching at a church", Clark says, "and had an altar call. In the prayer line was about 40 people. As I was praying for this person, I smelt this smell and I knew by the Spirit what smell it was. His name was homosexual. Whenever I get around a person that is an active homosexual, I can smell that devil. It's an

25

unclean spirit. When I was praying for this young man, I smelled that smell and said, 'come off', and God just body-slammed that kid to the floor."

In order to get the context of what Clark was saying, I reread the entire page, but the statement left me disoriented. It left far too many questions unanswered. For example, do other sins have distinctive smells? If so, what distinguishes them from homosexuality? Out of the 40 people in the prayer line, weren't any of the others sinful? Why did God "body slam" this particular young man? Does being slammed to the floor mean you're delivered from homosexuality? Was it His way of showing special disapproval of those involved in homosexuality or was it just the author's choice of prejudicial words? And the even larger question is what happened after the young man got off the floor?[2]

Did anyone offer to help him overcome his problem? Also, what does Clark do when he "smells" homosexuality in a public setting? Does he only deal with it in the comfortable surroundings inside the church walls? I'm sorry, but the questions are endless. I have seen at other times an almost violent reaction (by ministers conducting "prayer lines") to people who confess they are struggling against homosexuality.

The example, unfortunately highlights a gray area of ministry many homosexuals fall into when the subject of deliverance comes up. Clark's bizarre account of the "deliverance" of the young man maybe a lot more common than one might believe. Are homosexuals instantaneously delivered by the power of God or does it take a process of healing to bring them to wholeness?

Pentecostal churches, probably more frequently than other "evangelical" churches, place strong emphasis on deliverance theology.

There's nothing wrong with that, but there's much more to the story. Deliverance, in the Pentecostal thought, means, whatever your problem is, God will deliver you from it. And some have added that if you didn't receive your deliverance, it must have been because "you didn't want it bad enough." Well, I wanted to be delivered and fast before anyone found out.

The saints have been known to pray for hours for someone's deliverance or tarry until someone "came through". Usually someone laid hands on you and spoke in tongues, prophesied or rebuked devils. But still, so many people are lost, wandering around in the church looking for the manifestation of what someone told them.

Getting lost in the quarry of church-taught deliverance is no joke. I got lost my first day of school in 1970. I was a second grader and feeling very proud that I could walk to school with my older brothers. We didn't live that far from the school, just about 4 long blocks and a hop through some wooded trails, but when you're lost, it might as well be a million miles, you're still lost.

I have no idea how I got separated from them, but the sick feeling of being lost finally crept up on me. I ended up wandering around, up and down the same street, looking for my house. I went past Antioch Baptist Church and turned around at the corner and went by it again. I was very tired, scared and lost. I walked for hours looking at each house, hoping that I could get back home to safety away from the barking dogs.

Finally, a lady came out of her door and saw me sobbing. She asked me what was wrong. I told her I couldn't get home. She asked me what my name was and when I told her my last name, she said "Oh, honey, Ms Foster (my mother) lives right around the corner!" She felt so sorry for me. I was only one block away, but didn't know it.

27

Can you imagine wandering around the church for years, trying to find your way out of homosexuality? For many brothers and sisters it's a terrible reality. Revival after revival, prayer meeting after prayer meeting, but yet still lost. Deliverance seems so close, but yet so far away. The way out is simple, but not simplistic. We just need an understanding.

I believe strongly in God's delivering power. Yet, there is an *after altar* process that is sorely lacking in our churches. I believe this is why so many strugglers fall back into the lifestyle. Too much emphasis is placed on one night of ecclesiastical passion.

What happens when all the crying and snot-slinging is over? What happens when you get up off the floor or finish running around the church on your deliverance trot? What happens when the preacher has finished dousing you with oil and nearly knocking you unconscious? What happens after you have hollered three times to three people "I'm delivered, I'm delivered, I'm delivered!"? I'll tell you what happens. Nothing.

After the altar, seekers whose minds have been poisoned by satan's doctrine of sexual choice really need to be placed in a program which will begin undoing the work of sinful habits. When you consider that a person has been the victim of such progressive programming, without the benefit of any counteractive assistance, it becomes imperative that they learn how to be transformed by the renewing of their minds (Romans 12:3). Many strugglers may have ceased clubbing, gay friendships and sexual connections, but succumb to pervasive thought processes that have never been addressed.

The process of change is a difficult undertaking. Too often, we have settled for facsimiles of deliverance, instead of God's way. Please understand that jumping, crying, running, falling out, speaking in tongues and singing is not intended to renew your mind. But all of this occurs with frequency in the church because deliverance is a misunderstood word.

Deliverance comes because it is the fundamental work and pleasure of God. Just like there is no "almost saved," there is no "almost delivered." If we allow ourselves to categorize sin — homosexuality being the worst on the list— then we can easily slide into categorizing the work of God (who He delivers, who He doesn't). If sin is sin, then deliverance is deliverance. If we could deliver ourselves in any way, there would be no need for Jesus.

However, we must strike the balance. The church also carries a duty to the person coming out of homosexuality. Permit me to share a brief example from the Word, which will highlight this need for a whole touch: a touch from God and a touch from the church.

> *When an evil spirit comes out of a man, it goes through arid places seeking rest and does not find it. Then it says ,"I will return unto the house I left. When it arrives, it finds the house swept clean and put in order. Then it goes and takes seven other spirits more wicked than itself, and they go in and live there. and the final condition of that man is worse than the first (Luke 11:24,25 NIV).*

The reactionary conditions of crying, falling out, etc, prove nothing about deliverance. Under such stressing and distressing conditions that sexual identity problems bring, anyone will react in such a way. It is to be expected, but not confused with deliverance. Deliverance has four stages that incorporate a change in the soul, body, mind, and then, consummate all three.

CLEANSING YOUR SOUL

(1) The initial stage of deliverance brings about a **soul cleansing**. Homosexuality, like many other sexual sins is a sickness of the soul. That's why David said God "restores my soul". This is a miraculous inner cleansing of the soul, which only the power of God can accomplish. The indiscriminate blood of Jesus, shed at Calvary, sweeps over the soul and washes away the impurities of embedded, unnatural sexual passions! Hallelujah! Oh, what a change His power brings into our broken and shattered lives!

Why is the blood washing power of Jesus the most important and the first act of deliverance? Blood has always signified life. In fact God said in Leviticus 17:11, that the "life of the flesh is in the blood." Blood is such a powerful substance that once it touches, it can never be wiped away, it permanently stains like no other substance can.

Behind the scenes of daily living, blood dutifully performs many life-giving functions for the body. It transports nutrients from the digestive tract to the body cells; moves oxygen from the respiratory organs to the body cells, transports hormones, and assists in the regulation of body temperature.[3] Take away the proper functioning of any of these vital activities and the body will soon be lifeless. It's no wonder God says the life of the flesh is in the blood!

The physical significance of blood to the life of the body closely correlates to spiritual healing. The blood of Jesus establishes a permanent foundation of your freedom. From the moment it pours over your soul, you are a marked man or woman. You are bought with a price, forever stained and joined with the Savior. As you realize this, you will experience the unmatched joy of a prisoner made completely free.

You will instantly know that you have been declared righteous and holy. It's nothing you can do of yourself, it is the "righteousness of God" conferred upon you through simple faith. Why would Christ require us to do anything except believe Him, when He already knows that nothing we could do can free us from the power of sin? He calls us gently, even in our sins, saying "come unto me all ye who are heavy laden and I will give you rest." (Matthew 11:28). The beauty lies in the exchange: Your burden (sin) for His rest (deliverance).

LIBERATING YOUR BODY

(2) The second stage of deliverance involves **liberating your body** from the physical bonds of sex that has fed its need. Following the altar experience, the body must meet its initial appointment with sanctification. You must understand that although sanctification is a lifelong process of "laying aside the weight and the sin," an initial breaking is critical to moving forward in the recovery. Christ has declared you justified, sanctified and washed in the Spirit, yet you must now move to *act* as if the body is also free and justified. In the Spiritual realm, it is finished, but the flesh with its unredeemable nature (Phil 3:3), cannot be justified (Romans 3:20) so we are told to "reckon it dead." Paul taught strongly against the "flesh", but balances it with equally strong teachings about God's pervasive grace. Understanding the two in perspective to sin is very important to live above the challenges of life outside of the sin prison.

Homosexual sex is, as are other forms of illicit sexual activity, severely addictive, both spiritually and naturally. Praise God the anointing is available to destroy spiritual addictions, but it's your responsibility to break the natural bonds, by following the Holy

Spirit's guidance. IF you trust and obey, you won't find yourself easily going astray.

Far too many people mistakenly believe EVERYTHING is taken care of at the altar. The altar is simply a meeting place with Christ; a door whereby we enter in. But such misleading expectations leave them vulnerable to sexual ambushes which produce guilt and shame. Many will not readily admit to such failures which only complicates their situation. If there's one thing I've learned in my walk is to keep moving on. Don't let setbacks set you back.

Will it be difficult? I'll tell you the butt-naked truth. **Yes it will.** But remember who lives inside you and the source of your strength. We may live in faulty packages, but we are filled with a limitless supernatural power which gives us authority (exousia) and strength (dunamis) to overcome challenges. Because of this, you can be more than a conqueror! Why would God give us so much spiritual firepower, if there was nothing substantial to defeat? Just because circumstances are difficult, never means they cannot be overcome.

Sexual activities outside of God's keep you yoked to the death-curse of sin. This is why YOU must take the lead in destroying this particular bondage. For instance, if you are living with a lover or a past lover in a sexual arrangement, when you are delivered, you **must** get out of that situation. Waiting around and hoping the other person gets saved is spiritual suicide. Though God can keep you anywhere, you can't afford to live so close to the fire. When it gets hot, it will burn!

Getting away physically and getting away emotionally will give you the needed time to strengthen your love relationship with Christ.

Getting away from the heat of the past and its passion helps to freeze it's pull on you. The Apostle Paul teaches in Romans 6:13, "Do not offer the parts of your body to sin, as instruments of wickedness... (NIV)." Pastors need to understand that if two individuals have entwined their finances, transportation and living arrangements around a sinful relationship; the one delivered will need the assistance of the church to successfully make the transition of separation.

Why do we have halfway houses for drug addicts, teen runaways, prostitutes and ex felons, but believe that homosexuals should just jump out of the fire and live a perfect life?

TRANSFORMING YOUR MIND

(3) Changing your life means changing your mind. And according to the scriptures, this third stage of deliverance --transforming your mind--is possibly the longest and the most engaging. It is a joint effort of the Holy Spirit, the Church and you, the believer. In the Bible, the mind and the heart are closely related as God speaks His Word to us.

Holman's Bible Dictionary says that the word "mind" is translated from the Greek *dianoia*. It refers to understanding and sentiment resulting from the process of reflection. This gradual change of your thought process cannot be hurried nor will it fall out of heaven on you during spring revival. It is the essence of process and out of this process flows the issues of your life. Change is a beautiful thing to behold!

Although the transforming stage occurs over the remaining seasons of your life, it is nonetheless critical to the overall "success" of deliverance. In Romans 12:3, Paul carefully selects word pictures which convey a sense of continuity of the initial event. He says that we must be transform(ed) by the renew(ing) of the mind.

"Can the leopard change his spots or the Ethiopian his skin?" asks a Biblical writer. No, immutable traits like those can't be changed. Can you change 15 or 20 years of the same gender sexual thought process with one Sunday morning class on prayer? Probably not, but a regimen salted with spiritual teaching, mentoring and discipleship can bring change into the life of a same sex attracted person. Churches must understand outreach to homosexuals for long term effects must be specific and personal, not generic and mechanical.

Just how are you transformed by the renewing of your mind? The movement rate of the process may be different for different people, but the methods are always the same. This is where you put the horse back in front of the cart where it belongs. Many people struggling a-gainst homosexuality attempt to use the going to church, fasting, praise the Lord and reading the Bible thing as a means to the end. Some may be still sleeping around with old lovers. But these same people have not experienced the joy of truly having their soul washed in the blood of Jesus. Jesus called this experience being "born again."

The above (church-going, Bible-reading, etc) may reflect a facade of holiness, but out of order it is reduced to an endless puzzle. And truthfully, other people who see you engaging in these acts of piety will probably declare that you are "delivered", but behind closed doors, you know the real deal. Something is missing in your life and no matter how much you do all this stuff, you still slink back to your old ways. Well, your stuff is all out of order.

If you do things God's way, instead of the way your denomination thinks you should do or the way you saw your friend Johnny do it (who may be still slipping and sliding too), you can overcome homosexuality once and for all.

After you have made your way carefully, seeking God's face and hungering for His love and presence in your life, then it's time to get down to some serious Bible study. **You should be** in as much Bible study and Sunday School as you possibly can. You should be hungry to know the mind of God for your life.

You should allow the Holy Spirit to lead you into fasting and denying your flesh the pleasure of food, so that you gain greater sensitivity of His purpose for you. **You should be** jumping for joy during praise and worship! **You should be** getting involved in the life of the church and being obedient to those who have the rule over you. All of these things and much more, trigger motion into Christian life, transforming your living and understanding. If you are in a church where this type of seeking is stifled and discouraged, GET OUT!

This is what Jesus meant in Luke 11:24,25. I see fragmented teaching on deliverance that produces fragmented "deliverance". Jesus set forth all three stages in Luke. The soul must be swept clean, the body must be garnished and the mind sealed in order for deliverance to be holistic. Unless all components of deliverance are actively embraced and practiced, it can all be invalidated when the spirits return. There is no question about it. They will return.

PUTTING ON IMMORTALITY

The last stage is one that all Christians look forward to. Someday or night soon, Christ will return to the earth. He has promised that when He comes, He will take us away to be with Him for eternity. The Apostle Paul called this a mystery, yet it is a mystery revealed. The most astounding aspect is that there will be a supernatural, instantaneous, mass change.

> *Behold, I show you a mystery; we shall not all*
> *sleep, but we shall be changed, in a moment in*

35

> the twinkling of an eye, at the last trump: for
> the trumpet shall sound, and the dead in
> Christ shall be raised incorruptible, and we
> shall be changed. For this corruptible must put
> on incorruption and this mortal shall put on
> immortality (1 Corinthians 15:51-53).

Then, John further instructs us on this approaching hallmark, by telling us we shall be like the Lord:

> Beloved, now we are the sons of God and it
> doth not yet appear, what we shall be, but
> we know that, when he shall appear, we shall
> be like him, for we shall see him as he is. (1
> John 3:2)

All of our battles with homosexuality, cheating, dishonesty, division, death, pain, anger, will all be over. And when I see Jesus, the song says, it will be amen.

That day is coming, for sure, but meanwhile we must continue. But before you can claim any prize, you must endure. Don't churches teach that anymore? Have we forgotten that we must "run with patience the race that is set before us (Hebrews 12:1)?" It will only be the people who continue that will meet the Lord in peace and receive his coveted commendation of "well done good and faithful servant."

Far too many struggling saints, whom I believe do receive deliverance, become mired in so much discouragement, they get out of the race, some never to return. That word "continue" can really transform your life, if you will receive the wisdom of it. Sometimes the small things, the simple things can mean so much. What I'm trying to say, you may have heard before: YOU CAN'T GIVE UP!

Anything conditional means there are no free rides. That let's us know that God requires something of us, in order to activate the promise He has given.

KEEP ON KEEPING ON!

Consistent forward motion in our Christian walk is a challenge for us all. But thankfully we have a word from the Lord. That word is **"continue"**. Our purpose is to find out what God is offering us. Then if we want that offer, find out what we have to do to get it.

John 8:31 "Then said Jesus to those Jews which believed on him, if ye continue in my word, then are ye my disciples indeed."
What do I want? To be Jesus' disciple indeed.
How do I get it? Continue in His word.

Romans 11:22 Behold, therefore the goodness and severity of God on them which fell, severity, but toward thee goodness if thou continue in his goodness: otherwise thou also shalt be cut off.
What do I want? God's goodness to be upon my life.
How do I get it? Continue in His goodness.

Colossians 1:22,23 In the body of his flesh through death to present you holy and unblameable and unreproveable in his sight: if ye continue in the faith, grounded and settled and be not moved away from the hope of the gospel which ye have heard and which was preached to every creature which is under heaven whereof I Paul am made a minister.
What do I want? To be presented holy, blameless and innocent in God's sight. *How do I get it?* Continue in the faith.

If you are going to make it in your deliverance from homosexuality, you will have to learn perseverance. That's the key.

How many times have you heard or known of someone who

37

seemed like they were doing "all right", only to fall back into homosexuality? It can be a perplexing situation even for the more seasoned leaders among us.

A well known African American bishop who pastors a thriving church in the Midwest told me at a late night dinner in Chicago, that one of his music staffers had reverted to singing in gay bars. He confessed that he was disturbed and somewhat angry about it.

"Where is this coming from?" he asked, looking at me. He seemed sincerely reflective and concerned about the young man. "I don't just want to sit him down because that would not solve anything."

I had just finished hearing the Bishop speak at a church service. So I knew that he was a powerful preacher who understood human sexuality from the spiritual standpoint, but something about this was perplexing even him.

I confess it always grieves me to hear news like this, but we can turn it around. We can, if we set our hearts to do as the Bible instructs us to do. Perhaps, the most tragic thing of all is to hear some fellow saint remark "I knew they weren't delivered!"

The church taught me growing up to wait on my deliverance. However, "deliverance" from homosexuality in the black church can be very confusing. I had seen people delivered from drugs, drinking, backsliding, sickness and the likes, but never from sexual problems. For some unspoken reason, I just never heard of anyone being delivered from homosexuality. Was it because there were no homosexuals to be delivered? Hardly. So, according to the understanding I had, it looked like it was going to be a long wait.

I truly believed some powerful evangelist would show up one day, call me to the front of the church, fix his/her eyes on me, point a finger in my face and sternly declare, "Son, be loosed from that spirit of homosexuality!" That was my spiritual fantasy, my hope. Then, after I was delivered, every thing would be all right and even if people knew what my problem was I wouldn't care, because I would be free. No more thoughts, no more struggles, no more fear. No more inner conflicts. Isn't that the spiritual hope we all have to some degree?

I found out that you never have to wait on deliverance from sin! Deliverance from sin is possibly the only request God immediately honors. I don't believe God is a sadistic tease that would leave you in sin while you call to Him for help. If you call on Jesus, He will answer prayer! He's a prayer -answering savior, He will answer prayer!

As a youth growing up in the COGIC, I believed everything I was taught. I'm sure that other COGIC youths like myself believed that way too. How could we not? We were taught to pray, but did not understand the relationship of prayer. The prayers I prayed only made me more aware of the dichotomy of the church's words when compared to it's actions. They said God could do anything, but secretly they ridiculed and castigated homosexuals and even suspected homosexuals in the church. I remember one brother who, though he was married and had children, was noticeably effeminate. He was the type of brother that could "beat" a tambourine as they say.

One night after a church service I overheard one man saying to another that this brother was "funny" and that we should stay away from him. I'd always heard them say nothing was too hard for God, but I had never seen or heard of anyone testify that they had been delivered from what I was battling against. So I came to the (logical) conclusion that the more I had these thoughts, the closer I must be getting to hell. That didn't stop me from loving the church with all my heart.

Even with the conflicts, I felt special and a part of something I could not have in the outside world. I slowly became aware of my "heritage" and what that meant in terms of what I was going to be. I loved our music: bold, exciting and full of passion born out of struggle. I loved the leaders. (My little brother and I thought the Bishops were Bible heroes). I loved the way we danced our sanctified dance, free and uninhibited. I loved going to Sunday School to learn about God. I loved the preaching with its labored cadence and sing-song rhythms. Like it or not this was my world.

My church was sometimes dysfunctional, but I loved it. Mother Armstrong always sang "Walk in the light, the beautiful light" despite physical blindness. Sister Alberta Russell had a knack for donning bleached blond wigs and munching bites of cheese and crackers during the message. They were pieces in the sum of my life. But how does one love all this and yet reconcile the sanctified sanctimony that also existed in the church?

To complicate matters, there was a lingering mindset among black church folk that once someone became a homosexual, there was no forgiveness for them. They believed and taught strongly that God had "given them over to a reprobate mind." (Romans 1:28) And if God had given them over to a reprobate mind, they couldn't repent and if they couldn't repent, then they couldn't be saved. What a terrifying prospect facing a young teenage boy!

This tactic of Satan still plagues the black church today. This misinterpretation of the scripture has colored the effectiveness of combating sin without its cloak of secrecy. "But all uncleanness, let it not be named once among you ..." According to Greek Bible scholar, Spiros Zodhiates, the word "unclean" in Ephesians 5:3 means "moral uncleanness, filth, lewdness or any kind of unnatural pollution whether acted out by oneself or with another."

Homosexuality is moral uncleanness. The Bible did not say, nor was it the intention of the scripture, for saints to remain silent about it's occurrences among believers.

For me it was the crisis of a lifetime. I had done everything I was supposed to do to stop my thoughts and sexual feelings, but none of it seemed to work for me. By no means am I negating or mocking the power of prayer, fasting, praise and consecration in someone's life, but any of it, done without understanding its purpose, can produce spiritual sterility.

The year was 1977 and it was beginning to be the best of times for the fledgling "gay rights" movement, but for the church and its hard-line attitude against gays, it was undoubtedly about to be the worst of times.

My church supported Anita Bryant in her quest to turn back "gay" forces in Dade County, Florida. I remember the small offering we took up to send in support of saving the children. In a strange way, this eased the guilty pangs in my heart about my own sexuality. Now, somebody else was the bad guy.

41

4

Wounds from a friend

❧

omewhere in the course of my mixed up
feelings about sex and sexuality, I got a
girlfriend named Wanda. She wasn't my
first. I used to really like Kimberly, a white girl in my
2nd grade class and in then early on in 6th grade my
"girlfriend" (in my mind) was Brenda. But Wanda was
the first girl I really thought I was "serious" about.

I used to walk her and her cousin Pauline home
from school everyday. In my mind, it was just like that
old Cheerios commercial I used to watch. You know
the one that had the white kids in the front yard with
the white picket fence? They were all turning flips in
the falling autumn leaves. After eating those Cheerios,
they were the happiest kids in the world. Cheerios
made everything perfect.

The commercial had the most beautiful song you
ever wanted to hear. A song like, maybe Karen
Carpenter would sing. I'm too old to remember it
now, but that's how I felt when I walked Wanda home.
I just wanted to turn flips and sing that beautiful song.

42

Wanda and I got to her house late one day because I insisted on telling her I overheard my brothers talk about kissing. I asked her if she wanted to try. It took a lot of time and effort to finally convince her to give me a smooch, but she eventually let me get a little smack on the cheek, even under the threat of Pauline exposing us. When we got to her front yard I found out that Wanda's mother was not a happy camper. She charged out, banging the screen door open, a flowered apron tied around her waist. Shaking a big cooking spoon at me, she warned, "If you can't get Wanda home on time, y'all better ride the bus or something!"

I don't know what became of our brief, but blissful relationship, but when it was over, I went back to my conflicting desires and back to my fantasies. It's like that you know. When you lose what's real, you always go back to what you know. You always return to what's comfortable for you. The intermittent fantasies and struggles of my developing world welcomed me back from my brief vacation with Wanda. As the feelings inside me grew stronger, so did the deep sense of worthlessness.

Knowing how conflicting initial homosexual intimacy can be, many kids end up thinking about suicide. I don't believe the gay activists are lying about that. Sometimes the battles inside are so intense; it's just too much for them to bear. The question should be how do we direct these kids to God to heal the hurt of their lives?

For me, like many others, it seemed like I was trapped with no where to turn. What was I supposed to do? Who could I talk to? *Eventually,* I thought *somebody is going to find out about this and expose me.* I kept friends at a bare minimum, cause with secrets like that, you don't let people get close to you for fear they might reject you.

My church, Power House, was atypical COGIC, except a little on the ultra-traditional side. We had strict limits on social involvement: no movies, no football games, and no parties. We were even forbidden to attend churches of other denominations. I recall once being rebuked for joining a community choir and singing lead on "I don't feel no ways tired." It was at a Baptist church. But we did have a healthy dose of church. The limits of association imposed upon us kept us from some things, but also forced us into other situations.

I knew Ray (not his real name) for a few years, but only from a distance, although we attended the same church. He was responsible for my first homosexual encounter. Around my 10th birthday, my mother left Dwight and I at Ray's house because she was going out of town to church. We slept over his house because she would be returning late.

The three of us slept in the same bed, with Ray laying closest to me. As soon after the lights went out, I felt his hand snake onto my leg. My first reaction was to freeze and pretend nothing was happening. That proved to be a big mistake! My inaction emboldened him and soon he was fully fondling me. During the whole time, I lay still, caught between pleasurable sensation and gripping fear and revulsion. That incident led to other encounters.

Ray was quiet and unassuming and liked to play the organ. I forgot about his fondling and both of us spent many days at our church showing each other our simple church chords. He was much better at it than I was. Although he was a few years older than I was, we were friends. I continued to let Ray discreetly express his infatuation with me. He seized every opportunity to touch me. At first, I felt uncomfortable with it, but as time went on I rationalized it away and let him. Then my fear came back, and I hated it, however, it was too late. I had taken the bait.

I was a freshman now in high school and already I had managed to rack up a reputation for being a "fag," although I had not had sex with anyone. I got involved with the high school newspaper and worked on it for several years.

Some days at school were depressing. I never walked into the cafeteria during peak lunch hour. It was best to go in after the crowds thinned out. I was sure someone would yell, "hey, faggot!" I tried not to say too much to anybody, as I didn't want to give other students any ammunition to use against me.

I was thankful for one high school friendship with a quiet football player named Joel. He and I were friends for much of our junior and senior years. Joel was a neighbor of a lady from our church and he had visited with us on a couple of occasions. In school, he was always friendly to me. He sat by me in class. He studied with me in study hall. The relationship was unfamiliar territory with me. I thought he'd come to himself one day and say, "why am I hanging around this guy?" Despite my insecurities, Joel and I actually maintained a warm friendship all throughout high school.

Away from school, we could laugh and talk together. We cruised around town and talked about our dreams and hopes. I thought Joel's kindness meant I could tell him some of my secrets. I confessed to him that I thought I was gay. Joel sat perfectly still after my confession. He calmly asked me to drive him home, then got out of my car and never spoke to me again.

I can't accept the claims of the promoters of so-called gay rights. Especially when it comes to the attempted indoctrination of society and teaching kids to accept homosexuality. But on the other hand, I know the stark pain of losing a friend because of a sexuality struggle. No one deserves to be persecuted for something they're struggling with. When I say "struggling" I am referring to someone whose intent and desire is to please God despite the encroachment of homosexuality in their lives. Having said that, I refuse to believe any kid makes plans to be gay. But unless there is an intentional intervention by the people of God, the seduction of children to engage in homosexual acts will intensify dramatically.

I believe with all my heart and soul that if kids had more Christian parents, churches, agencies and ministries who openly addressed homosexuality and gave young people hope without condemnation, things would be better for many of them. We would see less suicides, fewer runaways and more emotionally whole kids. That's why I think that I allowed Ray's "harmless" advances at first. I was emotionally and relationally broken and didn't even know it. I had no idea what constituted healthy male relationships.

Ray always seemed as if he wanted more from me than he let on, but initially I never allowed anything more than a touch. Something deep inside me kept saying "this is not right", but I was much too close to the fire not to be burned. My unspoken feelings now had a name and a face. Soon, after those first few "harmless" touches from Ray, my life would take a turn down a long, dark road that I would not be able to get off until some 17 years later. It all began with my mother's devotion to the church.

Saturdays at my house meant church cleaning day. Mother was very faithful to the church and took responsibility for its cleanliness. That meant we were drafted, too. After cleaning the sanctuary one late summer afternoon, she left me to double check doors and lock up. I was surprised to find Ray in the rear of the church while I was doing my checks.

"Hey, what's up!" I said. He issued a nervous smile and kept walking. Then a few minutes later he called my name. When I arrived to see what he wanted, without warning, tentacle-like hands shot out with astonishing quickness. One grabbed my shirt collar and the other my neck and began pulling me like a crazed animal. I tried to stare at him, to connect with his humanness, only there was nothing there except a crazed and angry animal.

"Heeeeeyy! What are you doing?!

The small hallway in the rear of the church was transformed into a scene out of a horror movie, a nightmare no one would want to witness or endure.

"Noooo, let me go!" *How could someone who is supposed to be my friend do this to me?*

Beads of sweat formed on his forehead and nose as he yanked and jerked, huffed and grunted, yanked and jerked, dragging me into the adjoining room.

"Stop, let me go!" I pleaded with him. I was frightened. 13 years old and very scared and I started to cry. *He can't do this to me here, this is a church.* No matter what I did, thought, or said, I realized that no one was coming to my rescue.

This was a test of wills. The musty, dust-coated room sucked in it's breath and hid it's face as Ray and I tussled in it. The dirty windows and faded old curtains acted as accomplices, shielding us from any discerning view. As I went limp, Ray simply tightened his grip on my shirt collar and pulled harder. There was a bed about three feet away now, and he was determined to get me on it.

At the bed, he fumbled with my pants, unzipping them and pulling down past my knees. Then, my white underwear. His breathing was hard and labored from all the work it took to get me to this point. I gave up talking with him. I just kept thinking, this is a church, this is a church. This was my hopeless version of a prayer in my desperate heart of hearts that should have brought an angel or somebody to save me. But it was just him and me.

I sobbed louder, though it didn't stop him and did not seem to affect him in the slightest. *How could he face me at school after this?*

"Lay down!", he commanded. He was exasperated from the tussle.

"Lay back!" Behind me now, I heard his own pants unzip. He pushed me back and tried repeatedly to penetrate me. When that was unsuccessful, he smeared his body fluids on me. After he was finished, my attacker, my friend, without a word, walked out and left.

The assault left me feeling angry, afraid, dirty and despondent. I wanted to run to somebody and say "Look what he did to me!" but the fear overcame me. I waited until nightfall, sneaked home and then threw away all the clothes I had on so that no one would ever find out what happened to me. I swore it would never, ever happen again. But it wasn't quite over yet. Over the next three years, I was forced to bear Ray's relentless obsession with me. He milked my fears by threatening to tell everyone, including my mother, that I was a homosexual.

What I had experienced has become alarmingly common, but still underreported and addressed in our society of liberal freedoms. A comprehensive study done by Dr. Jim Hopper on the sexual abuse of boys in the US and Canada revealed that **1 in 6 boys is sexually abused before the age of 16.**

The laundry list of long term problems abused boys will have to recover from include:

"Anger, fear, homosexuality issues, helplessness, isolation and alienation, legitimacy, loss, masculinity issues, negative childhood peer relations, suicidal ideas and behavior, negative schemas about people, negative schemas about the self, problems with sexuality, self blame/

guilt, and shame/humiliation."[4]

Considering all of the resulting psychological and psychosexual abnormalities that occur when a young boy is sexually violated, churches need to invest into reaffirming boys as boys the way God intended. However, parents and churches frequently participate in the further wounding of young souls. We need to invest more in prevention and intervention.

A 21-year-old man in California I counseled not only struggled with homosexuality, but with anger against his parents (mainly his mother).

During our weekly telephonic sessions, he recounted his efforts to overcome his sexual feelings were routinely shot down with sharp criticism from his mother. She persistently lampooned his "faggot" friends and even taunted him with names like "punk" and "sissy." "She's a church missionary," he said.

My mother may not have been aware of what was transpiring in the night hours when she was working. Ray demanded that I meet him at different places, where he'd masturbate on me because I wouldn't submit to intercourse. We both still went to the same church. I wondered why the "saints" couldn't see what was happening. Why didn't God reveal it or had He and they were too afraid to do something? This had to stop. I was even willing to be exposed to stop it. Ray constantly wrote me letters about his "love" for me.

"Please," I begged, "don't write me anymore letters." If you do I'll take them to someone who can do something about it." I finally got the courage to demand it stop. Instead of complying, he wrote me one final vulgar letter, replete with hand drawn pictures of he and I in sexual positions.

Later that year, while on my first trip to the Memphis

convocation, Ray attempted to molest me in our shared hotel room. I hadn't guessed it would all blow up in my face.

This was the proverbial straw that broke the camel's back. After I gave Ray's letter to a youth leader, all hell broke loose. He was removed from his position, but his family harassed me. At school, they pasted crude pictures of devils on the outside of my locker and stole books from it. They insisted that I was the one who must have "seduced" him. Later, during a prayer service I felt that God had delivered me from my feelings and I tearfully confessed it. I'm not at all sure any one believed it.

The seeds of sickness, rebellion, anger and perversion were steadily growing up inside me. I continued going to church, but it was nothing more to me than a quagmire of religious rules and hypocrites. The experiences with Ray that I survived left my emotions scarred and set the stage for my deep mistrust of everyone, including God.

The second time I was approached sexually was at the age of 17 by the church's assistant pastor, a married man with three children.

The streets of my life
were already slick and
slippery, but then
Mike's unhappy
circumstances
fishtailed into my lane.
Everything seemed to be
spiraling out of control.

5

A Summer of twenty years: *Remembering Mike*

veryone remembers that special summer in his or her life while growing up. Hot Texas summers meant playing tag all day. Later we'd eat ourselves sick with watermelon. This summer, however, was the summer I was to meet someone very special and my hope was that it would never end.

When Mike ~cocky, streetsmart, funny and tough~ showed up in my life during the summer of 1979, I had no idea that he would affect me the way he did. I was scared of him at first. He was way too confident for me. He was the grandson of our church pastor, the late Rev. Isreal Echols. Mike lived in Dallas, but frequently came down during the summer to visit them. He had always come, but I hadn't always noticed him or wanted to.

I don't know how I ~sheltered, church-fed and sexually confused~ got to be friends with someone like him, but it happened. It was a hilarious indian summer. We sang together in the church choir that summer.

Mike's voice was like an oil drill: it went up and down. It was deep but changing, so it was difficult for him to control it. Side by side during the long nights of Wednesday choir rehearsals, we sang our gospel songs. Sometimes we got in trouble cause we didn't want to sing. Somewhere along the way, he started calling me "knucklehead." It was cool though, that was his term of endearment.

Once or twice, he and his Uncle Wayne came over to my house to eat my mother's cooking while we watched football. I hated football, but I was willing to watch a turtle sleep as long as it was with Mike. I'm not afraid to say he was my friend and I loved him. He meant a lot to me because he was carefree. That's right, he was an oasis for me. Sure he scowled when his grandma said things he didn't like. But he was young and all young people think the world revolves around them.

I think it was my open-ended struggle with loneliness and rejection that endeared Mike to me. My short time knowing him, caused me to be, later in life, very compassionate to anyone I saw as an outsider. Maybe it was a child who was left out of the game. Even at parties, people who weren't in the "in crowd" attracted me.

Mike's dancing gray eyes and sly know-it-all smile in a way said to me, "I know...but you're cool with me." He never called me a sissy or acted as if there was something wrong with me like other folks did. He made me feel, in his own way, like I was just one of the guys. Something I had always wanted to be, but could never seem to attain.

For someone like me, Mike's friendship was ground zero therapy. The last time I saw him, he was laughing, joking, full of life and looking forward to coming back to our little country town. That was the friend I remembered. The next time I saw him, he was lying cold and still, like he didn't want to disturb anything. His face had a faint smile on it, no doubt put there by the people who got him all dressed up. I had to say goodbye, even though he couldn't hear me.

That was the summer of his twenty years. Twenty years that God gave him and twenty years that Mike gave back.

The approaching pressures of high school senior status howled from a distance. This was the time in a young person's life where worry was supposed to consist of who was going to be the prom date or what college one was going off to. The streets of my life were already slick and slippery, but then Mike's unhappy circumstances fishtailed into my lane. Everything seemed to be spiraling out of control.

I knew something was wrong when I lumbered into the yard that day from school. Mother, my brother Dwight and a couple of other friends from church were standing there looking much too gloomy for such a beautiful day. Their faces told a story of bewildered grief. They didn't even attempt to prepare me for the news.

"Darryl, Mike is dead! His grandmother called and said he took a shotgun and shot himself in the head!"

"He's gone," somebody else said.

"Oh God!" I said to myself, "What is this?" Instantly, our summer together flashed before my eyes. My mind spun in rapid circles, out of control, searching for meaning and purpose in this. Around and around, pausing first at disbelief and then anger until...finally it shook me. Images flashed around me. I saw his smile, dancing eyes, saw us laughing together and joking about his singing. I saw him sitting engrossed in a Cowboys game, scowling because they had fumbled the ball...*again*. I saw myself trying unsuccessfully to get out of his playful headlock. Then my eyes burned with hot, confused tears. When I just couldn't make sense of it, I sat down and called his name over and over. "Mike...why? Why? Mike...why?" Oh, how my heart ached just for the privilege of saying goodbye to him.

53

I ran a thorough check of my memory, hoping it wasn't something that I said. Did someone say something to him about me? Why didn't he tell me he was having problems? I thought we were friends. Did he suffer? Who and what was on his mind as he was dying? I never got answers to my questions because the only one who could answer them was gone. I may never know why Mike left me or why the dull pain of his death is still in my heart after all these years. Perhaps he had a secret he needed to purge himself of. Perhaps the love he so unselfishly gave me, he could not give to himself.

But one thing I do know, it was a great summer. I loved him deeply for the friend that he was. I was very, very sorry he had to go. I was blessed to catch him at his best, at the end of his twenty years when his life was full of joy. If you've never had a friend like Mike, you need to get one.

Oh, and did I mention that I loved him?

EPILOGUE: SUICIDE

Suicide among young black men and women is no joke. Many times the stark pain of their death creates a chilling ripple effect on those that knew them and loved them, while the pain of their loss never quite subsides. Statistics show that this foul spirit has dramatically increased its stronghold among young people, especially (All statistics except those noted from Centers for Disease Control).

▶ A Centers for Disease Control (CDC) study released in 1998 found that From 1980 through 1994, suicide rates among black ages 15-19 increased 146% . [5]

▶ Suicide is an important and growing problem among black youths

10-19 years of age. From 1980-1995, in this age group, 3,030 black youths committed suicide. Suicide among black youths increased 114% from 1980 to 1995 (from 2.1 to 4.5 deaths per 100,000 persons).

▶The suicide rate among white youths was 157% greater than the rate among black youths in 1980; however, in 1995, the rate among white youths was only 42% greater than the rate among black youths.

▶The rates of suicide among black children 10-14 years of age (233%) and black teenagers 15-19 years of age (126%) years had greater percentage increases than white children (120%) and white teenagers (19%).

▶Firearm-related suicides accounted for 96% of the increase in the suicide rate among black children and teenagers.

▶The largest percentage increase in the suicide rate among black teenagers was recorded in the South (214%) followed by the Midwest (114%).

▶Among persons aged 15-19 years, firearm-related suicides accounted for 105% of the increase in the overall rate of suicide from 1980-1997. CDC unpublished mortality data from the National Center for Health Statistics (NCHS) Mortality Data Tapes. [6]

▶Each suicide intimately affects an estimated 6 people. Based on 745,000 suicide victims from 1971-1996, it is estimated that the number of survivors of suicides in the US is 4.47 million.

Suicide may be an accepted form of self-release and dignity in some countries, but in God's eyes, it is always a dishonorable and cruel way to leave this earth. Just like homosexuality among African Americans, self-murder still carries a dark taboo on its shoulders. Families who lose loved ones to suicide often react the same way as those who have lost loved ones to AIDS. When are people going to learn that unless you stop hiding, you will never get the help you need?

It's just like a sore, if you keep a bandage over it, it will never heal. But once the bandage is off, though it may be painful and somewhat uncomfortable, the body will begin its miraculous work of self-healing. Our community could save many lives if we would stop hiding the pain *and* stop hiding from the pain.

PART TWO

Life inside the tomb:
Making my bed with the wicked

Then he said to his disciples, "Let us go back to
Judea. But Rabbi, they said, "a short while ago
the Jews tried to stone you, and yet you are going
back there? Jesus answered, Are there not twelve
hours of daylight? A man who walks by day will
not stumble, for he sees by this world's light. It is
when he walks by night that he stumbles, for he
has no light. After that, he went on to tell them,
Our friend Lazarus has fallen asleep; but I am
going there to wake him up. Lord, Martha said
unto Jesus, If you had been here my brother would
not have died. Jesus said unto her, Your brother
will rise again.
The Gospel according to St. John,
Chapter 11, verses 7-11,21,23 (NIV)

6

A church boy finds the gay life

I no longer needed or wanted the church. As far as I was concerned, they had failed me. When I finally left the church, my home and my fears about homosexuality behind at age 19, I was ready for what the world had to offer me. I left with a deep hatred for the church, God, and my family. Somehow, I believed they had all abandoned me when I needed them most. Now, I wanted to do my thing; to explore my desires and live my life the way I wanted to.

It wasn't easy sneaking around to find out about the "gay lifestyle" in the little town of 7,000 I grew up in. There were no gay bars, hangouts, or discernable gay people. The one exception was a convenience store on the edge of town that stocked gay magazines. The first time I noticed the muscled, bare-chested magazine men peeking over the edge of the wood divider, I was shook with fear and excitement.

Immediately, I began devising a plan to get a magazine and gouge my starving desires with the pictures of nude men. I finally decided to stand outside the store until there was no one inside and no one driving up. Then, I would swiftly walk in, grab the magazine, push the exact amount to the clerk and head up the hill behind the store before anyone would know what happened.

The magazine was called "Honcho." I raced home with it and after locking myself in my room, poured over every page. Finished for the time being, I stuffed it in between my mattress. The next day, much to my dismay, the magazine had mysteriously disappeared.

I didn't know a thing about the "gay lifestyle", or even what it meant, however that didn't stop me from searching out all the possible connections I could. Trust me, deception comes easy to those who seek it. To me, this was a freedom like I'd never experienced before and it felt good! I didn't need the church or God to feel good. I didn't need their strict moral living standards. On the other hand, estrangement from my religious upbringing seemed ethereal. It was like a dream you wished didn't have to come true. The thing I hated most about myself was quickly becoming my passion.

In May 1980, I graduated from high school and immediately enrolled in junior college for the fall semester. I wanted to be somebody. I wanted to be an investigative journalist and write amazing stories for a large city newspaper. One amazing story was already writing itself. The 1980s proved to be a benchmark of social change, ushering in a formidable paradigm of sexual mores, even more dangerous than the free love pitfalls of the sixties.

No one was aware of the coming holocaust of HIV/AIDS. Death was lurking around every corner, but too many people were drunk with self satisfaction. No one seemed to notice that a generation of young men were poisoning their bodies and spirits with pleasure.

And so the cycles of my gay life began. Revulsion turned into curiosity. Curiosity became passion. Passion changed to obsession. Obsession ended up as...well, obsession. Just like the seasons of rain and snow, sun and wind, I learned to adapt to it's ways. Like Roberta Flack said, it was killing me softly...with its song.

7
Our brave
new world

*I*t was during that fall of 1980 that I died. The person people knew as Darryl fell by the wayside and someone new rose up. I was just a few months shy of my 20th birthday, on the brink, I concluded, of a bright future. I was optimistic at my prospects as a young man. I could battle the world's complexities and emerge victorious. I inhaled a deep breath of my freedom, feeling invincible, even a little cocky. Besides feeling like a new person, I was young, intelligent and free to be myself. A portentous thought came to my mind. *What could possibly stop me now?*

Then, on my very first venture out into my brave new world, I was hijacked, violated and murdered by my newly embraced sexuality. Don't bother searching, you won't find my death listed in any obituary archives. Don't bother yourself with checking, because I was just another young, black brotha who'd surrendered to the alluring, but deadly beauty of gay life.

No one in the church community really cared back

61

then because they felt a false sense of protection fueled by a desire to isolate themselves from the problems of "the world." However, if the church —especially the black church — believed it would find shelter from the calamity moving through the ranks of the unchurched, it was sadly mistaken. *Ultimately, homosexuality found a fertile new killing field in the pews and the pulpit.*

Bishops, apostles, pastors and ministers were struck down, dead from the pursuit of their sexual passions. Talented musicians, songwriters and singers were lost, their legacy flawed by secret sexual cravings. In the midst of this overwhelming devastation, church after church and family after family hurriedly concealed their losses. They put on false faces and made up false accounts of why their loved ones had left. The choirfests, midnight musicals and live recordings never missed a beat. They all knew the terrible shame stalking them would overtake them if anyone found out the truth.

HomoSINsuality wields a two-edged sword of guilt and blame, cutting each way across the grain of the human and spiritual spectrum. On the one hand, gays who refuse to believe in the inherent sinfulness of same sex behavior, cannot expect to stand before God with clean hands. But on the other hand, many people have been pushed into accepting their homosexual feelings as a result of the rejection and ridicule of the church. Homosexual activism has made its strides only within the last 50 or so years, religious gay activism even less than that.

Exgay author and past president of Exodus International North America, Joe Dallas writes in his book, A *Strong Delusion*:

> *Although there were some challenges during the first half of the century to the common belief that homosexuality was unnatural, there was no visible homosexual movement in*

*America until the 1950s. This is not to say that there was
no homosexual subculture before then; there was, and it
thrived. But the origin of the gay rights movement can be
traced to 1950, with the founding of the Mattachine Society (for
homosexuals of both sexes) and the Daughters of Bilitis (a lesbian
organization).* [7]

In a scant 52 years later, our nation has just about institutionalized
concepts of being "born gay" and homophobia. We have also accepted
openly hostile teachings which mock orthodox Biblical morality. Much
of the latter is coming from within the church world.

Has the church unwittingly aided and abetted the growth of
homosexual activist theology? To a degree it has. The church, believing
that if it just ignored gays and their growing demands, they would
soon go away. Who would have ever thought that open homosexuals
would be at the forefront of change in the nation's major
denominations? Ignorance embraced is a breeding ground for
rebellion and a little leaven leavens the whole lump.

I really don't think the church has lived up to it's mission of love
and acceptance. Too often, the church harbored the very predators
who plied their wicked crimes against us. The fathers have eaten sour
grapes and the children's teeth are set on edge. We are caught, it
seems, in a vicious cycle of rejection and hidden sin. That's not
condemnation from me, just the truth of the situation at hand.

I pray one day the church will conquer its fear and repent for its
mistreatment and persecution of homosexuals. I also pray that the
church will no longer embrace ignorance. The scripture says in Hosea
4:6, the people are destroyed when ignorance is accepted. They will
perish because there's no vision for truth, justice and freedom.

If true repentance happens in all sincerity, I believe God will
release healing both to broken homosexuals and to His church. I

know that this may turn some people off who nurture hardhearted views of homosexuals. They could care less if homosexuals came to Christ. They are oblivious to God's love for the sinner, even the "worst" of them. They can't see that all souls belong to God and it's not His desire that any perish. For years, God has communicated to His church how to deal lovingly and compassionately with homosexuals, but His words were flatly rejected.

The church, my Bible tells me, is the most powerful force on the face of the earth. Jesus declared that the gates of hell would not prevail against it. That's why it's frustrating to see the church swinging on an emotional pendulum. A pendulum that swings erratically from timidity, uneasiness and imbalance back to stone-faced hate. Far too often the cache of messages about homosexuality have contained nothing but condemnation. Bishop Carlton Pearson said that [the church] has convinced the homosexual of his sin, but haven't convinced them of God's love.

How can a body representing Love (God), engage in so much hate? If it's true that homosexuals are hell bound, then the church should be pulling out all the stops to reach them. Some leaders have stood by as passive as lukewarm water, while gays and lesbians (some of them their own sons and daughters) were driven out of the church. Gay churches are filling up with the rejects from the house of the Lord.

The Unity Fellowship Movement, (UFM) an aggregation of black homosexual affirming churches, placed a mocking greeting on their website. *"Whether your background is Baptist, COGIC, Apostolic, Catholic, AME...God is love and love is for everyone.",* it says. The truth is that UFM is attracting people who once sat in traditional churches, hoping to hear and see something demonstrated of love rather than judgment. Now, we are paying an awful price and reaping the fruit of the foolish behavior sown. Although many of them feel permanently alienated from the church, I also sense a deep longing by those same folk to return home. In their hearts, maybe *your* heart if you are reading this and feeling left out, is a desire to be who you long to be. Not gay, not a freak, not the object of scorn and ridicule, but a child of God. I want you to know coming home is only a prayer away. And like the good Father He is, He's waiting to receive you.

7
Closets and Clubs

ollege opened more doors into the secret life I searched for. The doors out of the closet revealed a worn pathway into gay clubs. At school, I slowly began to notice other people who I suspected were gay. They were the stereotypical types: masculine women and feminine men. I was a little turned off by their public candor, but secretly I wished I could be as "free" as they seemed to be. Later, I met many of them at the local gay bar.

Like most people experiencing something new, I stayed to myself, blithely observing and hearing. In a town like Waco, Texas, gay nightlife wasn't exactly public knowledge. As I pushed towards my goal, a battle still raged in my mind, but you see, my appetite was changing. I wanted to openly explore this forbidden and secret part of me now. I was tired of struggling against it by myself. I convinced myself that this was what I wanted.

I brought my churchgoing to a screeching halt and expelled it from my mind. Soon, without the spiritual roadblocks I was accustomed to growing up, I gave in totally to my desires. I quickly turned to the streets to find what I was seeking. I had no idea what to expect or who I'd meet. Night after night, I walked well into the morning hours. I changed my clothing; dressing in a way that would attract another man's attention. My thoughts had now become a brutal reality!

Christians who struggle against sexuality issues may not realize just how dangerous it is to ignore sexual thoughts. They grow inside you like a fungus. Some mistakenly believe that if the thoughts are not acted upon, they will eventually subside and even go away. Not true!

In March 2001 I was blessed to share my testimony at a Single's meeting at the Potter's House in Dallas. While I was speaking, the Lord revealed to me that some people in the audience held this misleading belief. I saw them in the Spirit desperately hoping to wake up one day and discover these tormenting thoughts had disappeared. I immediately and strongly denounced the spirits associated with this silent torment.

Later, when the Single's Pastor, Elder Tony Cummings allowed testimonies, one woman confessed that she had been tormented by these secret thoughts. Her dreams had turned into nightmares of her with another woman. As she stood, she began to weep as we prayed to God for a release from this tormenting spirit.

Another young man who called our ministry help line had the same problem. He told me that he occasionally had homosexual thoughts, but was adamant he would never "do anything". We talked several times about it, but he always assured me that he was saved and he had those thoughts under control. Then the calls stopped abruptly. Three weeks later, he phoned again to say that he had fallen sexually with an older man he'd met at a well known Dallas church.

The Bible teaches us that what is inside your heart and mind is just as important as what you do with your body (2 Cor 10:3-5). We should not only recognize negative thoughts are a threat to us, but we must do something to defeat them. Unchecked thoughts will soon lead to unchecked desires. Those desires, left to form a base of operation in your mind, will almost with a certainty give you fuel for action. Some things you do will shock you and have you wondering, "Why did I do that?" "How did this happen?" "Why can't I stop?"

I was too far gone to deal with my thoughts now, they had crossed the line into action and led me into the streets. Keeping what I felt inside no longer mattered to me. I only cared about satisfying the craving of my flesh. One night, on a downtown street, I met a young black man. His slouchy clothes and shuffling walk made me think he was a homeless person at first. My heart raced as he turned around to look at me once he passed by. I stopped and waited by the corner until he approached me.

"Got a cigarette?" he asked. He squinted his eyes and motioned to his lips.

"No, I don't smoke." I replied. We sized each other up.

"So, where you headed?"

"Just walking... on my way home."

I could tell by the look in his eyes that he wanted something more than a smoke, but I didn't dare pursue it. He eyed me warily. "My name is Ronnie... or Ron if you like. You wanna come to a party with me?

"What kind of party?" I asked. I had never been to a party before.

He laughed and gazed upward for a couple of seconds before he turned back to me. "Oh, we'll just go dance and have a good time," he assured me. Since he seemed like a nice guy, I went.

A gay club? This was an entirely different world for me. The sights, smells, sounds and sensuality of this portal into the gay life were a knockout combination of acceptance and enjoyment. Since this was my first time at a gay club, I was giddy with excitement. After Ronnie and I paid our admission fee, we entered a dark, smoky room. Like the outside of the unassuming building, the inside was long and rectangular. A small game room was to the left of the entrance and a bar lined the right side of the wall. This left very little room to maneuver in the press of bodies. People were crammed in wall to wall.

At that time it was Waco's only gay club, occupying a corner near downtown at 5th and Jefferson, a couple of doors down from First Baptist Church (NBC) and across the street from the old St Paul's Episcopal church. I was startled to see my boss, Gary, from the hotel where I worked as a night clerk there with his lover. He gave a surprising little laugh when he saw me and said, "Darryl, is that you? I thought you were gay."

Gay couples kissed each other and danced together. I had expected to see a bunch of old hunch backed Bela Lugosi types, but I didn't. It was full of young men and women: white college kids, professionals, country hicks, attitude laden black drag queens, and sprinkles of everyday folk.

Not one of them looked sad or ashamed about what they were doing or who they were. During that time, the club was fairly integrated, but when I returned for a visit years later, the owner refused entrance to me and another black friend.

It was an odd place, trying it's best to satisfy the mixed musical tastes of it's clientele. The club DJ tried to save *everybody's* life. You would hear "I love a rainy night" by Eddie Rabbit while boot wearing country couples two stepped, just as quick as you would hear Skky's soul drenched love hook "Call Me". Disco/high energy was shaping up in the clubs then and I fell victim to the techno-driven beats and frantic words of lust and passion. "So many men, so little time", sang disco diva Miquel Brown. Yes, that's exactly what I felt. The club scene was all at once the most boring, thrilling, interesting and suffocating place to be in.

My new friend, Ronnie, wordlessly pushed a Miller beer in my hand. I had *never* drunk anything other than soda and Kool-Aid...you know the soft stuff. But eager to look like I had it going on, I sipped on it. It tasted disgusting.

The heavy disco beat driving the music pulsated so loud, it felt like it was coming from inside me. As the beer slowly worked its intoxicating magic on me, I could feel myself warming to the "spirit" of the room. It was a slow and methodical seduction of my senses: challenging, questioning and then breaching the religion fortified walls I had built up. I would have never believed that I would be in that place at that time.

It's rather foolish to say what you will never do. I've heard people say that lots of times. But the truth is when you're on the enemy's territory, you become a SLAVE to your passions. And you will do whatever your flesh craves, because there are no restraints. Satan carefully prearranges and cultivates every detail of the night to inflame and stroke those passions. From the people you meet to the alcohol you drink, it's all one big setup.

In that setting, I overrode all sense of restraint I had known before. It just didn't matter to me. I was a fool in the company of fools and all of us were treading on dangerous ground. In gay clubs, all roads can lead to sex, if that's what you desire. Curious eyes peeped and peered at me, suspiciously, then, suggestively and invitingly. There seemed to be invisible, sexual notes written in their glances. To some, I sent a metaphysical thought or two back, others I ignored. Finally, I decided, *I'm in a place where I'm accepted and free to be myself. This is where I belong!* In just a short while, I had completely redefined my whole life!

As we stood looking over the crowd, a rather effeminate black man sauntered up to where we stood near the bar and eyed the both of us before asking Ronnie a question. He slid both of his hands along his hips, then raised them in mock surprise.

"Girrrrl", he cooed, "is this your new piece?" The loud music forced him uncomfortably close to us. Ronnie attempted to ignore him, and so did I, but it didn't work. He turned to me. His hands were on his hips again, studying me from obviously false eyelashes and half closed eyelids. Don't ask me why he kept thrusting his chest out as if he had breasts, but he did.

Nervously, I watched him out of my peripherals. He wore one of those stereotypical gay tied-at-the-waist shirts. I hated that look. He took out a long, slender cigarette and lit it. I hated the smell of smoke. He held his cigarette up and high in his right hand in a video ready "vogue" pose, while he decided what to make of me. I hated those contorted poses.

"Where you from?" he finally demanded. *Did I really have to answer that? I just wanted him to get his circus act out of my face.*

"I live here." I tried to avoid the insistent gaze of his bloodshot eyes. If I was Ronnie's "new piece", it didn't seem to slow his pick up game in the least.

"Is she treating you good? Cause if she ain't, you let me know and I can fix that!" With his message delivered, a toss of his head and some wicked hip swinging, he pranced off, disappearing into the sea of bodies. Due to my naiveté, I was really confused about the "girl" issue. I asked Ronnie about it.

"Oh, that's just the way these sissies around here talk.", he murmured with a dismissive wave of his hand. I still didn't understand why they called each other "girl" when they were obviously men. But I had a lot to learn about the gay lifestyle. The first thing I had to learn was the language.

That's another serious issue facing parents that should be afforded special attention. Young people are being seduced into homosexuality through its by-products of subcultural speech and lifestyle habits. The euphemisms, buzzwords and hyperbole of the homosexual culture are the hidden power vehicles behind youth-oriented slang.

Without realizing it, many youth who are not homosexual or even considering it, are deeply influenced by homosexuality. From the way they dress to what they say, there are many signs that popular culture is getting to them. For those who are at a sexual identity crisis, the allure and pressure to conform to what they see and hear is enormous. As I said before, when it comes to young people, it becomes a matter of prevention and intervention.

If you as a parent want to avoid traumatic surprises by son or daughter's proclamation of "Mom, Dad I'm gay!", I advise you get a basic understanding of what popular homosexual slang means and more importantly, what it means to the young person. It's one of seven signs (we'll discuss the other six in another chapter) of homosexuality in youth. But parents that are in the know can seek help earlier before other dangerous aspects of the "lifestyle" emerge.

Youth who are being seduced into "coming out" experience a powerful pull to emulate those who are currently portraying gay identities. It's no small accident that on television and the silver screen "wholesome" images of gays are popping up everywhere. At the same time, portrayals of Christians as fanatical hatemongers are on the rise. It's all about the image. These false identities are reinforced by witty jargon.

In the gay community, words drive the movement and shape ideologies that have propelled homosexuality from the closet to the spotlight in our society. The pressure to fit into this "lifestyle" means youth will be embracing new terms that might bewilder the average parent.

If your child has been incorporating words, you don't understand into their conversations, inquire in a non-threatening way what it means as a way of determining the source. I use the term "child", but keep in mind your child could be 13 or 30. I am in no way suggesting a witch hunt, but every parent should have a basic understanding of the gay community's word exchange. This will aid in active intervention and prevention of homosexuality in youth. A few of the more common terms are:

▶ *Trade* - a word which describes a man who does not consider himself homosexual, but occasionally has sex with other men. This male usually restricts himself to the penetrative role in a sexual liaison.

▶ *Queen* - a slang word used to describe an effeminate male, especially one who dresses in women's clothes. A drag queen (transvestite), though sometimes confused with a transsexual is a man who has not had any sexual reassignment surgery.

73

▶ *Fish* - a derogatory term applied to heterosexual women.

▶ *Top* - a preferred sexual position in a homosexual relationship. It is understood this role is the one of the penetrator. Conversely, the word "bottom" implies that the individual prefers a passive or receptive role in the male sexual relationships.[8]

▶ *Butch* - a term applied to either gay men or lesbians who portray a masculine appearance.

▶ *family* - a term used to describe gays in a familiar circle as in a family relationship.

▶ *In the life* - a phrase used often by African American gays which denotes active homosexual living.

Much to my surprise, I discovered that being new on the gay scene makes you hot property. Eventually, everyone was asking my name, where I was from and whom I was dating. The attention drove me wild.

On the dance floor, the altar of gay socialization, somebody handed me a little brown bottle called a "popper" or "rush," a word for the inhalant amyl nitrite. One gyrating man next to me jammed the little brown bottle up in his nostril, inhaled deeply, then passed it to me. I followed his example and instantly, I felt my head about to explode with a super-high feeling of ecstasy.

Throughout the rest of the years I lived as a homosexual, I racked up a serious addiction to the little brown bottle. I always took a bottle to work and anytime I went out. Eventually I sniffed it so long that my nose and upper lip turned raw at times.

It didn't take me long to sell myself out to club life. I heard the refrain to a disco song blaring on the giant speakers..."so many men, so little time." It must have been the Waco club's theme song.

All that week, I could think of nothing but how good it felt to be where I was. I couldn't wait for the next Saturday night! I bought a new pair of tight Levis, a button down shirt and some new cowboy boots (that was the country/preppy look). I wanted to make sure I wasn't looking like a newcomer my next time around. Until the Lord saved me years later, club life held a tremendous grip on my spirit. Without it I felt I couldn't live a happy life. I'm not saying all gays are club addicted, some are actually anti club. But it was a stronghold that took God's supernatural power to break its grip on me.

Though Ronnie had introduced me to the club, I soon found him boring and ditched him the following weekend. It wasn't hard to make friends, that's what the gay life is famous for. If you feel rejected by others, you will surely be accepted in their ranks. A couple of drinks, a little dancing and a person can easily lose their apprehension about being in a completely homosexual surrounding.

My next outing was just as exciting as the first. I was a lot more relaxed this time around. I drank several beers and a shot of liquor. Over a period of time, club life forced me into a gradual increase in drinking, especially when I became anxious about "scoring" for the night. It began with one beer, but later I would drink anything and as much as it took to boost my confidence when approaching other males.

That next Saturday night I returned to the club alone. I drank, but I wasn't drunk. When time came to go home, Ronnie offered to have a friend of his drive me there. The soon to be rapist was introduced to me as Larry. I had not seen him before, but I felt this was okay, since this was my new "family," our code word for gay. We both climbed into his old car and took the near wordless 10-minute ride to my south Waco apartment.

Just like an unsuspecting fly, I stumbled right into the spider's web. My first steps out to so-called freedom were met with sexual violence from someone in the "family". It was by far the most traumatic and humiliating thing that had ever befallen me. I understood this to be friendly territory, but it was the farthest thing from the truth. How ignorant and foolish I was!

After the 200 pound rapist dropped me off, he came back 15 minutes later. He pleaded with me through my closed door to let him in. "There are certain people at the club I have to warn you about", he said. He said Ronnie was one of those people.

"Please," he begged me, "I wouldn't feel right, if you didn't know." That's why I let him in. I never thought he would rape me and I trusted him.

Soon after he got into my sparse apartment, we sat down opposite each other and our conversation began. A creeping awareness told me that he wasn't there to tell me about anyone. All of his questions were personal and about me. I noticed the lust in his eyes and heard it in his voice, but I didn't know how to deal with. If you've ever been in this type of situation, male or female, you know how unspeakably terrifying it is. This was for real! Before I knew it, things had escalated and he grabbed me around the neck, half-dragging me to a back room. Unlike the experience I had at 13, this ended in intercourse: brutal, painful and deeply humiliating.

My first reaction when it was over was to just cry and cry, something I had always done when I was traumatized. It wasn't supposed to happen this way. I hadn't done anything wrong to anybody. I just wanted to enjoy my life. Several "life shots" flashed before my mind's eye. *God wants you to come back,* a quiet voice said. However, my pride and rebellion wouldn't let me admit that I had already messed up my life.

Anger overtook my self-pity. I grabbed the telephone to get the police, but then reconsidered. I didn't want my family to know. For God's sakes, not now! And I really didn't think that the police would take it seriously. In the following weeks and months ahead, I changed. I developed a hard, callous attitude as a result of the recent and past hurts that I'd endured.

From now on, I would play the game, too. The gay life was about hurting people and I decided to master it. The anger inside me began to poke its head out. I couldn't get this guy, I didn't know him at all, but I would get even someway. Unfortunately, most of the destructive behavior was self-directed.

I "got even" by doing as many wild things as I could. I went to house sex parties, which briefly led me into the orgy scene. These extremes quieted the hurt on the inside for a short time, but there was a monster living on the inside of me that I could no longer control.

Down on my luck and ready to be kicked out of my apartment, I moved to Houston just before Christmas 1981, to do a stint with a "magazine sales group" which was in reality a prostitution/theft ring. Inside me, anger and humiliation battled for supremacy: one wanted violence, the other depression. Between the two of them, I was headed nowhere faster than I realized.

Our false MO was simple. We pretended to be college students working to pay our way through college. For every magazine subscription we sold, a financial contribution would be made on our behalf. Or so we were told.

9

Hustling on empty

ouston was gearing up for Prince's "1999" tour and I arrived just in time. Prince's sexually explosive songs and seductive character typified the attitude of the times which he enunciated in the refrain of his title song: "party like it's 1999". My favorite song was the Barclay's "Hit and Run." Its ironic refrain, ~"you played your game for fun, now you are the only one,"~ seemed to prophetically mock me. I made choices along the way that caused me to sink deeper and deeper into the hole satan had dug for me. Still, I truly believed I could make it on my own, I just had to be smart.

I became fast friends with Stacy, an on again, off again drag performer from Alabama. Together, we explored Houston's gay Montrose district every chance we got. Sex was everywhere. It was a spirit and we worshipped it willingly. We danced, partied, and drank ourselves silly. It was all so much fun then, so exciting

78

to be gay and open in an atmosphere where no one condemned us. It was quite a welcome change from the harsh glare I felt the church offered. But none of the fun, sex or partying answered the real, masked needs in my life.

If the question, "what's a good church boy like you doing in a place like this?" comes to your mind, then it's the same question I asked myself frequently at points along my journey. It was as if I was stuck on a defective ferris wheel. I was too afraid to get off and too ignorant to know how. My association with this thug operation was proof of that.

Two weeks after my arrival, Mr. Banks, a gruff-voiced man and the group's head "pimp" summoned me. When I came into his gloomy office, he dropped his head and squinted at me over his glasses.

"I know you're gay," he announced with a smacking tone. "But I want you to know that's ok by me as long as you do your work and have fun." I stood in front of him stoically, neither denying nor affirming his statement. I wasn't sure about his motives for this "speech" and I wasn't about to give him anything to work with. Although no one ever came out and said what type of organization it was, I started having serious doubts about remaining with them.

I grew increasingly paranoid after seeing others abused. A female was backhanded so hard in the van one night her glasses flew off her face and she cried. Stories about Frank's (the driver) temper, especially when someone didn't make their magazine sales quota, were frequently whispered about.

Our false MO was simple. We pretended to be college students working to pay our way through college. For every magazine subscription we sold, a financial contribution would be made on our behalf or so we were told. We were instructed to choose any college, but to make sure that we knew familiarized ourselves with it and the city it was in.

We were put out on the streets or dropped in various black neighborhoods usually until 2 am. Black neighborhoods were chosen because Mr. Banks believed them to be the most gullible, especially if we sounded "honest" about our purpose. We hustled money and sometimes sex. Stacy and I were paired together; I'm sure purposely, so he and I were always looking for male customers to hustle.

I had only a few dollars of my own. We were rationed those few dollars out of the money we took in although we were told the rest was being "held in an account" for us. The walls of this organization began to close in on me. Finally, fearing for my life, I confided in Debra, one of the females who seemed gay friendly. I decided to talk to her after several secret attempts to contact my sister Myra, who lived 45 miles away failed. Debra's words confirmed my worst fears.

"Darryl, he's (Banks) not gonna let you go." She stared at me wide-eyed on that cold January night in Houston. We both stood there on the street shivering, wondering what to do. I told her I was getting out. I was scared, but adamant. She agreed to help me, but would not go with me. Leaving was a risk I had to take, and one she would not take.

We hurriedly discussed my options since Frank was known to ride around and check up on you. Debra agreed to cover for me, to buy me getaway time. She promised to lie to Frank, telling him that I went to another house while we were out (which was against the rules) and she never saw me again. "Child, I'll just tell them you probably met some man you gittin' it on with." she said with a sly look. She flashed me one last white toothed grin and slipped away, half running.

Everything I owned was at the hotel we stayed at. I was a long way from Buffalo Speedway on the West Side. I had nothing except the clothes on my back. I decided to attempt a few more quick sells and use the money to buy a bus ticket back to my mother's house. I slipped into a nearby neighborhood and walked down the street looking for a friendly house. It was already 9:30 at night so I had to hurry to make this happen.

Then, at one corner, I noticed a COGIC church. The building sat there like a Biblical "city of refuge." A rush of relief flooded me, because I knew that if I contacted someone from the church they would surely help me. I went to the house directly across the street and nervously knocked. For some reason, the door was open and the outer glass screen door allowed me a peek inside. A middle-aged woman lumbered to the door but stopped short and stood away from it when she saw who I was.

"Can I help you?" she said cautiously.

"Yes, mam. My name is Darryl and I'm from Waco. I'm in trouble and I need to call my mother and let her know I need help. Can I please use your phone?" The words tumbled out, partly out of fear, partly out of relief.

The woman said nothing. She didn't have to, her eyes said it all. Mistrust.

"Do you know anyone who is a member of the church across the street?"

"Yeah, me and my husband is.", she answered.

"Well I grew up in the COGIC and my grandfather founded a church and my mother is saved. I thought that someone could help me out to get home." I kept having images of Frank riding by. I wanted and needed to find some common ground with this woman. But she balked at my words and never moved an inch closer to the door.

"I can't let nobody come in my house." she finally said. I knew it was over. The thought came quick. I don't know if it came from me or the devil on my back, but it came quick. *The church never wanted you anyway.*

Nevertheless, I had to get away. I had no time to waste. Another desperate sell netted me 22 bucks. I literally ran for several miles to the downtown Greyhound station. For all I knew, Debra could have betrayed me.

Once I arrived at the bus station, my eyes darted constantly, ready to bolt if I saw anything out of the ordinary. The station was filled with ten gallon hatted Mexicans and fidgety blacks. One young black mother held her child. She was rocking the child nervously and looking around. I wondered if she was running away from somebody, too. Several of the Mexican men stood in a corner like undercover agents. Forty five minutes after I arrived, the first service announcement for Marlin came over the intercom. I clutched my ticket and kept my eyes glued to the entrance door.

Then, at last, I boarded the bus, on my way home. As the trees and highway lights became a distant blur with the bus's acceleration, the tears of shame, failure and defeat streamed down my face. I remembered my mother's pleading words before I left: *"Baby, don't go. You don't know what those people will do to you."* But I was going home now. It was all right now, I kept telling myself over and over. I was going home.

The bus arrived in Marlin around 2:30 in the morning. I was the only one who got off there and as soon as I did, I headed towards the only real home I knew. It was a long walk of uncertainty, more crying and the chill of the night air. Mother was already at her night job, so I climbed through a back window and went to sleep on her bed. By the next morning, I awoke to find her sitting quietly by the bed.

I found out that life in the streets was no game. Bad choices will always lead you down a dangerous road. But the fear was not enough to change my ways nor was it enough to satisfy the deep seated unmet emotional and relational needs that continued to railroad my life. Though my mother welcomed me back and took care of me, I soon grew dissatisfied and craved the club life again. I left again in the summer of 1982, a couple of months before my 21st birthday.

Trying to move on past the bitter situation in Houston I managed to squeeze out of, I was driven to do something to satisfy this longing in my heart. I know now it was for love, but love only meant one thing in my mind. Sex. My searching for sexual partners intensified and was marked by promiscuity. I revived my streetwalking in search of a "pickup."

This became a nightly affair as well as hanging out at some local "straight" clubs in search of a "straight man." Picking up a straight man (trade) for sex was considered a real conquest in gay life. That's when I met Jeanetta, Foo-Foo, Andy and Garry. All of us different, but at the same time alike in so many ways.

We formed our little gay "southside gang" because we all lived on Waco's southside across I35 from Baylor University, smack dab in the middle of the Mexican community. We were definitely a sight to see: four black gay men and a black woman who was always in our business. Can I tell you a little about our goofy gang of misfits?

My friend Jeanetta was the extra large single mom of two small boys. Jeanetta was no nonsense, maddeningly funny, boisterous and full of life. We became good friends after she figured out that I didn't want her. I'd quit my job earlier because my female supervisor Lynn, found out I was gay and stuck a knife in my face threatening to kill me if I ever "tried to get her husband." No job meant no money for rent, which meant no place to stay. So Jeanetta invited me stay with her until I got back on my feet.

Fu-Fu, was the clown of the group. Tall and lanky, with slits for eyes, he was the first one to experiment with wearing makeup and women's clothing. He proudly called himself "Sustah." He was Jeanetta's nemesis. She said from the very moment that they met, Fu-Fu was a drag queen, but we didn't believe her. It was the set up for a long tussle between the two of them. Of course, she proved right. Fu-Fu kept us laughing hysterically at his late-night "street cheers." He said he always wanted to be a high school cheerleader.

Andy was mixed Black and Spanish and very attractive, but extremely vain. It was Andy who told me later of having a secret affair with a local minister whose family was blue blood COGIC. The minister later died (most believe) of AIDS. Although Andy was very petite he constantly was in competition with Garry, who fancied himself a world-class, high society diva. As insecure as a person could get, Garry always smoked long cigarettes and acted as if he had no time for the "little people" of the world. At first we were all amazed with Garry's grand stories about his sexual escapades with well known people in LA, that is until we found out he'd never been to LA. We all at one point lived together until things started to fall apart.

I eventually quit school due to a combination of finances and incessant partying. My friends, with problems of their own, one by one fell away. With hopes of my career derailed, I knew it was time to make a real change in my life.

> "I had grown accustomed to gay life in the civilian world, but I was amazed at the number of homosexual men and women in uniform. Just like my initial introduction into gay life when I first heard the term "family", we also referred to each other as "family.""

10
Homosexual?
Not me!

ncle Sam and the promise of a change intrigued me though I never intentionally wanted to join the military. But in October, 1982, I temporarily hid my homosexuality so I could get into military service. There was no "don't ask, don't tell" policy when I enlisted. Homosexuals, if exposed were quickly dismissed from the service with dishonorable discharges. My heart pounded against my chest in the recruiter's office as I sat reading the question repeatedly: *Have you ever had sexual relations with someone of the same sex?* I mulled over all the possible ways I could phrase my answer to the question, but in the end I marked "no."

I never really meant to join the military. I only wanted to see what my chances would be if I just took the test. I knew that once they discovered I was gay, it was a dead end. But, God somehow moves you towards destiny in the strangest ways.

I'm sure the sergeant saw my anxiety. But I passed all entrance exams and was set for a new season in my life, one that would bring with it sweeping changes in me and how I viewed the world around me.

Military culture was a complete shock for me! As I mentioned before Charles, Lance and Robert had all served or were serving in the military. I knew it would be hard, but some of the disciplinary tactics used by the drill sergeants in basic training could seriously be classified as torture! The "drills" first order of business was to scream, yell and swarm like angry bees until they broke down our defenses (sounds a little like satan's tactics). I knew I was in trouble when I saw some of the tough guys (or at least that's what they said) from Boston and New York break down and cry.

Nothing was sacred or off limits to the drills torture tactics! A favorite subject was....you guessed it!, our mamas. The word faggot took on a whole new meaning and the threat of physical violence shook the weak ones among us to the core. Although I had to sneak off and drop a few wet ones myself, I hung with it and finished my training. I couldn't believe it when I received my diploma March 19, 1983 from the Air Defense Artillery Command at Fort Bliss, Texas. I was a soldier!

I'll never forget the impact my senior drill, Sergeant First Class (SFC) Harold Richardson, had on me. He was a gaunt, bowlegged, little white man who didn't weigh 20 pounds soaking wet. I think every basic trainee remembers one drill they identified with. For me, it was SFC Richardson. He was spit shined and starched from head to toe. When I first saw the way he walked (actually swaggered), talked, smoked and cussed like a soldier, I immediately knew I wanted to emulate him. Hey, sorry, that's the army way of life.

He was tough and he knew how to train you. Tough though he was, he still seemed to care that you were the best soldier you could be. Out of the whole group of drills, he was Mr. Perfection. If you didn't do something right, Sgt. Richardson possessed a terrifying arsenal of punishing exercises like the "dying cockroach", to get you on the right track. Thirty minutes of those would make any trainee want to sell his soul to the devil to get it over with. I knew I was his favorite in a weird sort of way.

"Foster!", he barked at me once, "son, if your head wasn't stuck so far up your dark side, you might be a good soldier!"

After I completed basic training, I was assigned to Fort Monmouth, NJ, then to Fort Lee, VA and finally ending up at my first "permanent party" duty at Fort Campbell, Ky. The army gave me the opportunity to see a little bit of the world and I did. After 8 months at Fort Campbell, I volunteered to serve in Honduras, although there was armed conflict at the time between Nicaragua and Honduras. I spent 4 months on that tour.

In early 1984, when I returned to the US, I received orders to the Multinational Forces and Observers (MFO) which was deployed in the Sinai desert near the Isreali border. The Force was primarily peacekeeping, but the region sizzled with terrorism and hostility over the Isreali occupation of Palestine. My assignment there took me all over the historic lands of the Bible, a true blessing. For several months I served as a staff driver for the MFO Headquarters detachment. My job was to drive the chief of management into the Gaza Strip to take care of contracts. I completed one year of service in the Sinai and returned to a brief stateside assignment at Fort Benning, Georgia, the first of two.

I enjoyed all of my assignments and learned a great deal from being a soldier. My homosexual involvement increased in service, though I understood that I could have been kicked out if it was discovered. Upon returning "stateside", I resumed going to gay clubs as soon as I could and eventually became familiar with numerous gay service members.

I had grown accustomed to gay life in the civilian world, but I was amazed at the number of homosexual men and women in uniform. Just like my initial introduction into gay life when I first heard the term "family", we also referred to each other as "family." They ~we~ were everywhere and in all ranks. I reunited with John, an elementary school classmate, who was gay. After my assignment to what the Army called "permanent party", I thought I was the only gay soldier in the world until I met Frank, a guy in my company at Fort Campbell. Frank was well connected and quickly introduced me to the inside world of military gays. I felt proud that I could keep my homosexuality a secret and be a soldier. I thought I had the best of both worlds.

My desire was to excel in everything: from inspections to being one of the first in my company to earn the coveted "Air Assualt " wings from the 101st Division School. I never wanted to be known as a gay soldier, just a soldier, and so I felt I always had to prove myself as better, tougher and as "gung-ho" as possible.

The all male world the army provided suited me just fine. Once in my life I had been somewhat fearful and apprehensive of women. I tolerated their presence, but on most occasions, refused to interact with them. Later in my military career, I developed feelings of superiority over women. I despised the women who were with men I wanted.

I wished that I could live on a woman-less planet and my hatred and jealousy of them continued to grow. I know now this was a setup from the enemy. Those feelings progressed until I literally despised women. This hatred fit in perfectly with the other objects of hate I had set my guns on. My standard line was "Females have nothing to offer me", and I was absolutely sure that women were inferior (sexually, emotionally, mentally) to men. They could not give me what I thought I wanted and needed. I had bought the lie that sexual intimacy with men was what was normal for me and women were abnormal, so I had no problems hating women who got in my way.

We (homosexual men) contemptuously referred to heterosexual women as "fish" and shunned them unless we were forced to deal with them. We derided them, laughed at them and dreamed about taking the men we saw them with. I had never been sexually intimate with a woman before and at that point in my life had no intentions of ever doing so. To me, women were useless competition to be painted away with my broad brush of hate.

Everywhere, during my service involvement, I found willing sexual partners. Some were married, some not. Some said they were in "committed relationships" with other men, and others who were just looking for quick sexual highs like me. I really didn't care. So-called long-term relationships weren't my thing. My deep mistrust of everyone prevented that from occurring. Even when it did occur, my brokenness and insecurity would soon derail the relationship.

The molestation at age 13, the violent rape at age 19 and all of the other sinister pre-conditioning of homosexuality was now etched into the fabric of my soul. Those situations had already knitted shut my authentic need for love. I had already closed the door on God. Closing the door on people was only a few footsteps away. I wasted

89

those eleven prime years of my adult life chasing the fantasy of homosexual intimacy. At certain times when I wished with all of my heart that I was not gay, something would whisper to me. *The intimacy you are pursuing is not the intimacy you need.* I felt powerless to stop what I was feeling and even more helpless to find out how to stop. The truth is I chose not to believe it.

The pursuit of homosexual intimacy is like a carrot on a stick cruelly held out before an unsuspecting mule. Like the mule, you chase and hope; hope and chase, chase and hope, always with the lure of love a fleeting breath away. Then as you reach out to get it, it's snatched away and whisked to another place. Though I felt secure with my life, there was no security anywhere. The men I wanted and the men who wanted me, had one thing in common. We could never gain what we sought in each other. That intangible factor of true love refused to be held with those hands. I had money, I had game, and could get I sex hookup with ease. But I didn't have Jesus, the man I really needed in my life.

11
Can I tell it?
Praise break!

*A*nd they overcame him by the word of their testimony and by the blood of the Lamb because they loved not their lives unto the death (Rev 12:11).

When I was young, growing up in the church, I told my manufactured testimony. I learned it by memory. I hope you can rejoice with me, that through all of my failures, error and rebellion, God has given me a new testimony. I ended up being an eyewitness at my own trial. Out of the mess I made, God truly gave me a message. This didn't come off the church's assembly line testimony factory; I learned this one in the vicarious school of life without God.

We are stewards of the testimony. That's right, we are managers of the testimony of Jesus Christ. It's not ours, because the focus of a TRUE testimony is the great work of Jesus. We are charged to tell anyone, everyone of the excellent work of Christ in our lives. I like to think that I am a living resume for Jesus!

91

My wife and I have received so many letters, cards, emails and telephone calls from precious people —some of them deeply conflicted about homosexuality— since we started on this walk of faith. They are all so very moving to me. I want to share a portion of one that is representative, both in tone and content of what we are hearing from the "field."

January 21, 2002
Dear Pastor Foster,
I was so blessed as I read your testimony of all
that you went through and God brought you out. I
read it on Saturday evening after surfing the net.
I was so blessed. I have heard testimonies but
truly you have a testimony. What an awesome
God we serve. Tears rolled down my eyes as I
read through your pages. At some points I cried
like a baby. I think it was a healing process for me
Pastor. I believe that God is going to give you
platforms in the future to share what the Lord
has done.
Many people don't understand all that takes
place with that type of lifestyle. I strongly believe
that God is raising up more people who will
address this area because the enemy is trying to
attack a vast number of young people while the
church sits around and wear large hats and deny
the power of God. Truly, I want to encourage you
to stay close to God and be encouraged. God is
with you and he has great things in store for you. I
even saw you on TV while I was reading your
testimony. The word tells us that eyes have not
seen and ears have not heard nor has it entered

into the heart of man. The things that God has
prepared for them the love him and have been
called according to his purpose.
[namewithheld]

We may never know the extent of what God will do through our confession of His awesome work in our lives, but we can be assured that He will use those words to bless someone greatly.

In the midst of my own precarious bouts with happiness, I battled with deep depression. It felt like I was at times, being swallowed whole by some unseen force. The extreme feelings of isolation manifested in me as an overpowering desire to use my body to attract others. After the depression lifted, I tried to "make up" for it by promiscuity.

I've got so much to praise God for! He has lifted me up out of the miry clay and set my foot on a rock to stay. I need to tell my testimony because I know it is my weapon of defeat against satan. What he meant and devised to destroy me, God has used to lift me up and out. He made my enemy my footstool. Sharing your testimony releases you from the fear of what the past did to you. Sharing your testimony takes away the weapons of intimidation and instead empowers you with boldness. It may be a quantum leap of faith to get to that point, but once there, it brings great healing in your life.

Can you imagine selling yourself to sin? That's what I did. I lost my will to care about what happened to me. As I reflect back on my fragmented life, it is a miracle of great proportions that I am not dead. During those 11 years, I can count on one hand the times I used a condom or was even asked to use one. Death was all around me. Thousands of young men who have done less than I are now dead, yet God spared my life!

AIDS was something I never even remotely considered would

happen to me, and I lived and conducted myself according to that false belief. That's right, so-called safe-sex was a joke to me. I wasn't interested in using condoms and neither did I want my sex partners to use one. After 11 years of uninhibited male sex in all of its varied and degrading forms, I did not contract AIDS. I was a fool then, but I'm favored now.

I felt I came into the gay life at the height of its decadence and fixation with "free sex." Then, AIDS was just a nasty rumor in gay cliques. People whispered about who was getting sick and fears about it crept around gay communities like the black plague. I was no different from any of the ones whose names are nothing more than a memory on a quilt.

Maybe some of those who have died were your brothers, fathers, friends or lovers. But by divine grace, God spared me from the shame and death of AIDS. I know what I deserve. I deserve to be dead. The wages of sin is death. I don't talk to God about justice, because I know what I rightly should have received. God purposed that I should be saved alive to tell this story of His ability to salvage the most damaged of lives.

With shame, I confess I frequented gay bathhouses (24 hour male sex rooms) in Frankfurt and sex clubs in Tel Aviv. Oblivious and blind to the danger, I've tramped the streets of Nashville, Houston and New York City, sometimes near naked. I offered my body, as a sinful sacrifice to whoever would worship it. I've been so intoxicated that I didn't know where I was, who I was having sex with or how many, yet God let me live! In the midst of my hell-bent desire to destroy myself, He shielded me and allowed me to walk away physically unharmed. This, to me is the unexplainable depth of the agape love! This is grace!

Like a sexual vagabond, I subjected myself to sexual encounters with unknown men in public parks, restrooms, and in many places that decent people would not dare tread. I stand completely amazed that some people think that I should not tell people where God has brought me.

Why should I be silent when it was God and not people who set me free? I heard the Bible say, let the redeemed of the Lord say so! When God brought Isreal out of Egypt, Moses commanded them; "Remember this day, in which ye came out of Egypt, out of the house of bondage for by strength the hand of the Lord brought you out from this place" (Exodus 13:3).

When I first shared my testimony at my church back in 1996, another Christian told me that my testimony was "my business" and everybody didn't have to know it. What a lie! I have had several encounters with both those who professed and those who didn't who felt that exhomosexuals should keep their mouths shut. One woman wrote to the local newspaper saying she didn't know "creatures" like me existed!

I don't want anybody trying to gloss over all the hell I went through! The Bible doesn't try to paint pretty pictures of the sins of Abraham, David or Peter so why should we try to pretend we haven't had our hands in the stank pot? People who have been battered by sin will appreciate and identify with others who have survived the road to hell and lived to tell.

I attribute this attitude to the enemy who is angry that he was not able to kill me in my sins. There have even been threats of lawsuits against me for telling what God has done for me. I have been ostracized by the denomination I was born in and cold shouldered at church meetings because I refuse to keep quiet about the goodness of God in my life.

I feel like blind Bartimaeus. The more the try to shut me up, the louder I will cry out HE DELIVERED ME! HE SAVED ME FROM HOMOSEXUALITY! The glory of the Lord cannot be contained, it is to be a sweet refrain issuing from our hearts to bless and encourage others.

It still puzzles me that after all my vivid and extensive experiences as a homosexual, some homosexual activists find it convenient to deny I was ever gay. I've been told it's something I made up, a lie concocted for political reasons.

Maybe they're right. Maybe I wasn't really gay, I just lived out the lie satan tricked me into believing. No matter what people say, I know that God delivered me from the snare of the fowler and He protected me from the deadly pestilence! I can say like David: A thousand fell at my side and -CAN I TELL IT UP IN HERE!?- ten thousand at my right hand, but it did not come near me. God shielded me from the destruction and sudden death that surprised many and laid waste in the noonday. Hallelujah!

No, I didn't deserve one iota of His love, but He did it just for me! I wasn't worthy enough to touch the bottom of His shoes, but He lifted me anyway. You may not understand it, but He loved me with an everlasting love! He pursued me with passion! He purposely spared my life as a memorial to His infinite goodness and grace. Praise God! This is why I serve Him today. I WILL bless the Lord at all times and His praise shall continually be in my mouth! Glory to God! I know the Lord had His hand on me. He knew the thoughts that he had for me, thoughts of peace and not of evil to bring me to an expected end.

I cannot explain with any sense of rationale or reason why God chose to protect me from death. I can recall so many times, where I was in harm's way and could not have saved myself if I wanted to. We can never boast of anything, because it is truly the will of God that keeps us alive.

Romans 2:4 asks a question which I will paraphrase, "Don't you know that the goodness of God leads to repentance?" In other words, God ALLOWS us time in our mess because He is mercifully granting us time to repent. The Bible says "He is patient with you, not wanting anyone to perish, but everyone to come to repentance" (2 Pet 3:9) NIV.

While I was in service, I barely escaped criminal investigation (for homosexual conduct), but now I understand that the goodness of God was leading me to repent. I narrowly escaped falling over a 300 feet embankment in the Sinai desert. That was the goodness of God pleading with me to repent. Once after a fight in a gay club, a man put a knife to my throat and threatened to kill me on the spot, but miraculously a friend knocked the knife from his hand and we escaped. The Holy Ghost said "that wasn't your friend, I did that, because my goodness wanted you to repent!" The goodness of God kept on leading me.

I was within moments of having sex with a man with full-blown AIDS (he died a few months later), but God sent someone to divert me and I did not do it. He dispatched an angel with a flaming sword to stop this insanity. All I can say is that the goodness of God was leading me to a place of repentance. As the scripture says, "Don't you know that?"

How about you? Is God's goodness leading you to repentance? Has he been pleading with you to turn to Him? Because the Bible said it, I know that He is. If you sense that He is, stop right now and repent, ask Him to forgive you and turn away from your lifestyle. There is a way that seemeth right unto man, but the end thereof are the ways of death (Proverbs 14:12). Then when lust hath conceived, it bringeth forth sin, and sin when it is finished bringeth forth death (James 1:15).

So you see my brother and my sister, the road you are on, though it may afford you temporary pleasure, leads to destruction. Unless you get off and take the access road to God's will, you will meet with a tragic end. Why die when you can live?

If you want to live, stop now and pray with me. Once you have prayed, lift your hands and begin to rejoice because God has heard your prayer.

Father God, touch heal and deliver me, right now. I come to you in faith just as I am, believing that the price for my sexual struggles was paid in full on the cross. Forgive me and heal the hurts of my soul. Lord Jesus, I give you my broken heart and renounce my rebellious spirit. Fill me with your love and make me a new creation. You alone have the power to give me true freedom. In Jesus name, Amen.

12

The game of love

*B*eing in the "lifestyle" taught me that the game of love was played hard and fast. You needed to constantly update to remain attractive. Youthfulness was a universal symbol of virility. And if you wanted to be in the game, if you wanted to someone to want you, you had to look the part. You had to know how to move and what to move with so you didn't look old. You learned to swallow your hurt quickly, because the next man could be snatched up while you were grieving over the last one.

Due to my mixed up emotions, I developed a hard, insensitive attitude towards everyone, even "lovers." I played a terrible emotional game of love. By that, I mean I would draw others into my confidence with smooth talk and hungry passion, then discard them when my sexual appetite was appeased. I'm sorry that I perpetrated my sins through them.

As a person, I had a valid need for love, but I was

too afraid of being hurt again. And I didn't know how to love because Christ did not live on the inside. So I was left to my own devices. At times I outwardly said, "I don't need you!" But secretly I hoped that *this* man or *that* man would be the one I could find true happiness with. Many of the men I came in contact with were just as broken and disillusioned as I was.

Yet, we all played the game well. We passionately pursed social masculinity because it was our idea of success in an unfriendly world. Yes, you could look good, have your body in the best shape, dress well, drive a nice car and have money in your pocket, but that was part of the game of love's illusion. All of it was simply a cover for the burning need to be accepted and loved by other males. Attempts to find anyone to fill that God-shaped void in our hearts other than God will always be a relentless, barren pursuit. We were all looking for the ever elusive "Mr. Right". Or if we couldn't get him, then maybe his best friend was interested. As Earth, Wind and Fire mused, "That's the way of the world!"

My three year assignment in Germany was filled with new people, new places and new sins. I intensified my drinking and hard partying whenever I could. I was stationed in a small military post about 30 miles south of Frankfurt, the German version of New York City. I discovered a freedom and culture of sexuality there that I had never known in the states. I would have never dared kiss another man openly, hold hands in public or embrace, but I did it there.

I was assigned to a combat arms unit whose mission it was to help deter so-called Soviet aggression, therefore I spent a lot of time in the dreaded "field." The training missions could last 30-45 days at a time. When our unit completed these strenuous missions, the party was on. It felt so good to be young, black, single and gay! The hottest spot on the planet was a Frankfurt gay club called No Names. No Names was all black, all military and all gay. A few celebrities (sorry, I can't give those names) even partied there occasionally.

After a steady succession of different lovers, one night stands and sexual escapades, I finally thought I had fallen in love with someone who I'll call only by his last name, Walker. Opposite from me, impetuous and extroverted, Walker had a quiet, strong spirit. From the very first time we met, I had deep feelings, yet I was extremely apprehensive that someone would come along and take him away from me (another side effect of the lifestyle). When he and I were out together, I was so proud. But beneath my outward show of pride was that unsettling fear. I constantly guarded him against advances from others.

It was a terrible way to live. It's also the hidden heartbreak of gay life. I believed Walker was my Mr. Right, and I went to great lengths to prove that to him. If it is true that what goes around, comes around, then I got my dues. Our relationship ended in a sharp argument that plunged me into more promiscuity.

True "commitment" in homosexual relationships is fiction. At its best, it is fragmented and vicarious. If gays told the truth, they would admit that true relational commitment simply does not exist. Many heterosexuals may wonder how two people of the same sex can love each other, or if that is even possible. I felt what I understood to be love, but I cannot find any justification for it in God's Word. The "love" (eroticism is no substitute for love) between homosexuals can be deeply emotional and perhaps intense, but falls into the category of man's fallen nature. Christians should never engage in ridicule of homosexual love because it hinders our mission of reconciliation.

I'm not implying heterosexual relationships are picture perfect.

The truth is homosexual relationships can never reach the standard of God's intent for sexual expression. Because of that, looking for completion or satisfaction in someone of the same sex is a doomed expedition.

13
Brother to Brother

*D*uring my last year in Germany, my brother Robert, whom I had not seen in over 10 years, contacted me. He had been in Germany a long time since the end of his military service. Robert had gotten married to a German woman in the southern city of Stuttgart. He managed the local Non-Commissioned Officers (NCO) club and now had a son of his own. I was glad he was doing well, though I was guarded about what I said. He seemed glad to talk to me and we agreed to meet. He decided to come and visit me at my kaserne (army post) near Giessen, some 300 miles from him, because I didn't have a car.

I was somewhat reticent about it, but I really wanted to see my brother. He and I had not spoken in a long time and there was a period in my life where I did not care if I ever saw him again. It was his voice when I was young that rebuked me when I wanted to play ball with him and his friends. Out of all my brothers he seemed

103

to be the most derisive when he called me sissy. My only memory of him was that I hated him and was sure that he hated me. Nevertheless, I decided that I would meet with him. I also decided that I would not hide my sexuality from him. I got "butterflies" in my stomach worrying about what he would think of me after I told him I was gay. He would just have to deal with it.

Our meeting wasn't as dramatic as Jacob and Esau's reunion. When Robert and I finally met up on a Friday night about 7 o'clock, a rush of pent up emotions escaped from me. I'm not sure he knew why I cried, but the tears were a tremendous relief for me. Just the fact that he had come all this way to see me, said a great deal that he did not hate me.

Robert and I went to the club on Kirchgons kaserne to drink a few beers and try to talk about our life growing up, and what the military had done to the both of us. I wondered if he was thinking about my sexuality. We managed to laugh a little and drink more beers that loosened both of us up considerably.

I remembered that I wanted to tell him I was gay and the beer gave me a false courage to do so. We went outside of the club and stood looking at his yellow Mercedes. *Everybody* in Germany had a Mercedes.

I blurted out, "There's something I need to tell you. I hope that you will listen cause I don't know any other way to tell you." The darkness helped me conceal my anxiety. "I want you to know I am gay." I said. I was surprised I actually looked him in the eye as I said it. But it was his reply that shocked me.

"You're still my brother." he said, "And I'm still going to love you gay or not." My brother hugged me and gave me one of those handshakes that the straight men did. It was, for me an awesome moment in my life. My "gayness" did not bother him; he was more concerned with me as his brother.

Robert and his wife Carmen, had possibly become accepting of gays. A couple of months after our initial meeting, I called him to ask if a few friends and I could come and visit him in Stuttgart. He said yes. To my surprise he took us to Kings Club, a gay bar in Stuttgart and allowed my lover and I to sleep together in his home.

The lesson I gained was that acceptance from family is a powerful benchmark in the life of a homosexual. It is however a pendulum that can swing to the good as well as the bad. My brother's acceptance of me as his brother, gay or not, was a good thing. I wouldn't encourage anyone, however to help or encourage that individual to live as a homosexual, knowing the inherent dangers in that lifestyle.

I began attending church for a while, eventually I joined and stayed there about seven months, however, I did nothing to change my lifestyle. I found it difficult because although I desired to be in the church, I could not or maybe should say did not want to give up the partying and sexual trysts that were dominating my life. I briefly played the organ for a small COGIC chapel service on the kaserne (German word for barracks) where I was stationed. One Sunday morning after a hard night of partying in Frankfurt, I was sitting on the organ and a small boy came up to me during offering.

"Bro. Foster," he said, "your eyes sure are red!" "Son," I replied, "Bro. Foster has been up all night." I realized I just didn't want to hypocrite in church any more. If I was going to be a sinner, I would just get out and do it to the hilt.

After those three long years in Germany, I returned to the states. It felt good to be back in the USA. In 1989, I was sent back to Ft Benning. I'd served there briefly before for about 8 months, so I was very familiar with gay life in Columbus and in Atlanta, 100 miles to the north.

I'd narrowly escaped an embarrassing investigation by the Army's CID (Criminal Investigation Division) and potential dismissal from the Army for homosexuality while stationed in Germany, so I was thankful for the chance at a fresh start. At the same time, I was fed up with having to hide my sexual preference. I was tired of the front I put on in my attempt to convince certain people that I liked women, when I really liked men. I was forced to lie and conceal my whereabouts and associations. There was a real possibility of being kicked out of the military for homosexual conduct. The need to experience some freedom from that cloud set me up for another chapter of failure and upheaval in my life. I wanted to do my thing and laugh at the people who were always prying into my personal business.

That's when I was approached by a lesbian acquaintance with a very strange proposal.

14
An Indecent Proposal

arriage was never a fantasy, or a dream, not even a remote desire in my life during my gay days. I never believed I would be married and least of all to a lesbian. I wanted nothing at all to do with any woman. But like a dangling piece of delicious fruit, it hung before me: an offer I couldn't refuse. Could I, a gay man, marry a lesbian, pretend she was my wife and we all live happily ever after? Sure it would work, right? I would not have to fend off any more questions or looks from the guys who insisted on knowing where I was going or who I was seeing. I toyed with the idea for several days.

My barracks roommate, King, was a smart, wisecracking playa from Philly, but he was saved. The brother apparently had a fetish for classy shoes. King owned so many pairs of shoes, I thought he was running a shoe store out of our room. As I got to know him better, to me he was some kind of churchaholic wanting to share his joy bottle with me. I always refused, ignored him or didn't come in from the night before until I knew he'd gone on another church binge.

"Foster!" he'd say in that nasally insistent East Coast voice, "come on man, get up and go to church with me!" His addiction was temptingly infectious, but I resisted. See, I had a plan. I was getting out and coming out. I met someone who could help me do that. I knew Shirl because she cooked up a mean egg and cheese omelet. That's what I had for breakfast each morning after our 2 mile fitness run. She was a supervisor in the dining room of our battalion "mess hall" where she worked. I had my suspicions about her sexuality, but it really wasn't my business. We happened to bump into each other one night at the club out on River Road and started to talk. To my surprise she was very pleasant. Over a few glasses of my favorite rum and coke, she laid out her plan like a battlefield commander. She was intent on taking Annie, her war spoils, her civilian lover, overseas with her.

I watched her short jheri curl ringlets shake and wiggle as she talked. Her hair was changing colors with every light show switch on the dance floor behind us.

I thought it was simple enough, and without much discussion, agreed to do it. Getting married would supply me with extra money, a quick way out of the gossipy barracks atmosphere, and a good cover for my secret life. It sounded like a real smooth deal to me.

Shirl's plan was for Annie and I to get married at the JP. Once we were married, I would get Annie a dependent ID card so that she could go overseas with Shirl. She had already received her orders for overseas assignment, so we had to act fast.

What we planned to do was nothing unusual. Many army gays were doing these "arranged" marriages to keep others from suspecting them of homosexuality. The military always gave married service members more money to live off-post. The extra money would be mine to keep. That was our agreement. Annie and I would live together for a couple of months, so in case someone came by, our front would be in place. *This is my life, I told myself, and finally I'm going to live it the way I want.*

On February 19, 1990, Annie and I went to the Justice of the Peace, across the border in Phenix City, Alabama, said our phony vows and got married. We were both awkward, jittery and nervous. Shirl stood by as our only witness. The JP jokingly remarked that I should have, at least, had a ring for my new bride. We did it quick, on my lunch break from work.

Annie and I followed our deceptive plan. We deceived our parents and others who didn't know the real deal about us. I bought a $12.99 ring and put it on my finger (sometimes the wrong one). The next week, I called home and broke the news to my mother. She gasped in disbelief! I told her I would send her a picture of my wife in the mail, which I did.

Happiness was finally within my reach! And no one could stop me, not even God! I remember when I felt convicted by the Holy Spirit, telling God, *"I don't care if I go to hell! If I go, I'll just go!"* I believed it was His fault anyway for not helping me when I needed it. Now, I didn't want to hear anything from Him or any of His people.

MARRIAGE OF CONVENIENCE

Annie and I moved into a gray trailer home right outside the rear entrance of Fort Benning and set up house. Right away, we began having our separate lives in one house, which caused a great deal of friction. When she had her lesbian friends over, I was angry and left. I hated them. When I brought my male friends over or a sex partner, I threw her out. Our tidy little arrangement fell apart fast. I discovered Annie was a cheat, a liar and drug addicted. Besides, she and Shirl, like most lesbians, fought constantly. Although I drank, I didn't want tons of liquor in the house and we argued constantly about it. Since this was a sham marriage, we never consummated it.

Annie refused to work and demanded that I support her until Shirl took her to Germany. The two of us didn't have one thing in common and it showed. After a month, the situation was in shambles and I would have done anything to get her out. I'd married a liar.

One evening, during a hard rainstorm, she insisted that she needed to go and buy food for the week. "I need some money" she said, sticking her hand out. I reluctantly forked over $75 and mentioned a few things I wanted her to get for me. I was totally unprepared for what would eventually happen later that night.

I was in the back room watching television when suddenly there was a loud banging on the front door. Annie was back: soaking wet, incoherent and screaming! I was so shocked, I could only stare at her! What could have happened? She lunged inside the house when I opened the door.

"Darryl, I've been robbed and raped!" she gasped. Breathing heavily, she stumbled in and fell onto the couch. I took a quick assessment of her condition: clothes partially torn, no bruises or cuts anywhere. As far as I could see she was just overexcited and wet.

"Call the police!" she moaned. I was reluctant to do this because, though I couldn't put my finger on it, something about this picture was not right. Shrugging it off, I punched in 911 on the phone.

"I believe my wife has been raped", I said bluntly into the phone.

When the voice on the other end pressed me for answers, I got defensive. "Just get somebody over here!," I screamed at him. About 25 minutes later, two policemen and an ambulance were there. Red and blue lights flashed repeatedly like a scene out of *Cops*.

The police calmly questioned me since she was unable to speak. "How long have you been married?" "Does she do drugs? How long had she been gone?" I was uncomfortable, not to mention embarrassed. Later after all the drama, The police said that she had not been raped and that she was on drugs. She apparently had went to buy drugs with the money I gave her, but the drug thugs jumped her and took it. She concocted the rape part to prevent me from finding out about the drugs.

After the escapade with Annie, I quickly demanded she get out. Our, two-month arrangement was up and I was ready to be free of her and the whole mess. And as per our pre-nuptial agreement, she moved in with Shirl.

Around this time I tried desperately to jump start a sexual relationship with Chris, a former friend from my first tour at Benning. He and I had been mutual friends, but this time things were different. I believed I was deeply in love with him. There was only one problem: the feelings were not returned. Undeterred, I pursued him constantly, hoping he'd change his mind. I'd let him keep my car, gave him gifts and money, but he remained uninterested sexually. In my mind, he belonged to me. My jealousy and rage at not securing a relationship with him began to eat at me. I became so violent and vindictive that I would purposely endanger myself, hoping that would get his attention.

One night I was told by a friend that Chris had gone to Atlanta to party with another male. I was livid. *How dare he mess around on me!*, I thought. I jumped in my car so consumed with rage, I swore that where ever I found him, that's where I would kill him. The rage eclipsed everything rational within me. I paid no attention to the car's gas gauge, which was near empty and subsequently the car ran out of gas 45 miles out of town. I never made it to Atlanta. Once again, God had slowed the pace of the enemy's destructive design for me.

Two months after I gotten married, with all my plans to be a happy, openly gay man, the first thoughts of suicide began to creep in. Was this how it began for my friend Mike?

My fragile dreams unraveled at breakneck speed. And in typical Darryl fashion, I made a grab for something to steady myself. Not even the frequent "sexcapades" brought me the satisfaction they once had. I was still heavily into the club scene, but neither did it provide peace of mind and satisfaction. I couldn't seem to shake the growing uneasiness in my heart. I decided my solution would be to "settle down", get a steady lover and be faithful to him. A few weeks later, I found him.

PART THREE

God speaks to the dead man:

Coming out alive, shedding the past and healing for the future

"Where have you laid him? He asked. Come and see Lord, they replied. Jesus wept. Then the Jews said, See how he loved him! Jesus, once more deeply moved, came to the tomb. It was a cave with a stone laid across the entrance. Take away the stone, he said. But Lord, said Martha the sister of the dead man, by this time there is a bad odor, for he has been dead there four days. Then Jesus said, Did I not tell you that if you believed, you would see the glory of God? So they took away the stone. Then Jesus looked up and said, Father I thank you that you have heard me. I knew that you always hear me, but I said this for the benefit of the people standing here, that they may believe that you have sent me. When he said this, Jesus called out with a loud voice, Lazarus, come out! The dead man came out, his hands and feet wrapped with strips of linen, and a cloth around his face. Jesus said unto them, Take off the grave clothes and let him go. "

The Gospel according to St. John,
Chapter 11, verses 34-36,38-44 (NIV)

15
A time to turn
꧁❧

God was calling my name, but I didn't hear His voice. He was pleading with me to turn to Him, but I ignored Him and continued focusing on my selfish wants and desires for happiness. And that's precisely the position the enemy stubbornly attempts to force us in, a place of want. When want is a product of your own fleshly desires, it will never be filled. The flesh always craves more than it can ever have, thus creating a deep cave of lack in your heart.

> *The obvious works or desires of the*
> *flesh are these: sexuality immorality,*
> *impurity and debauchery, idolatry*
> *and witchcraft; hatred, discord,*
> *jealousy, fits of rage, selfish ambition,*
> *dissentions, factions and envy;*
> *drunkenness, orgies and the like*
> *(Galatians 5:19 NIV).*

I was 29 years old now, living alone in that same gray trailer home. Satan renewed his campaign to destroy

114

me by reminding me of all the old hurts and rejections. The attacks seemed to intensify with each waking day. Because my soul was damaged, it was easy for the holes in it to release the pain into my heart and mind. He repeated over and over to me that no one loved me. I was a outcast and a failure and no one wanted me in their life.

"Yeah", his wicked voice sneered, "you can find a sex partner anytime you want, but none of them love you." The awful thing about it was I felt he was right.

I became convinced that despite of all I'd said and done over the last 11 years, my life was worthless. No one could have imagined how awful it was to be something you hate but feel so powerless to change it. This realization fueled the hate inside me. I became a man of intense hate. I hated myself, my family, the church and most of all, I hated God. I knew that I had done too much to be forgiven.

The more I hated, the more my life lost its value in my eyes. One night I took a cab back from the small gay club I went to on Friday and Saturday nights. The cab driver talked to me about suicide. I don't remember exactly what he said but later I realized it was another message from satan prompting me to accelerate and finalize my plans.

I thought I had found my lover for life. Once again, he was my "Mr. Right." I got involved with him because I wanted to chase away the growing feelings of being unloved and unwanted. That was until he started stealing my clothes and money. I had broken up several friendships to "get" him and now I was paying for it. After I let him move in with me, he steadily took advantage of me. The bliss lasted a fleeting week. The climax came when he stole my car and was gone for three days. When he returned, we got into a violent fight and I called the police to have him removed from my house.

THE LIFESTYLE BECOMES A DEATH WISH

It was Holy Week 1990 and I had already wasted a decade of my precious life wrapped up and pursuing all that I could as a homosexual. I confess that I enjoyed, even relished being homosexual at times, and did not want to give it up. That's the reality and the smooth deception of sin. The Bible tells us in Hebrews 11:25, that Moses chose to suffer with the people of God rather than *enjoy the pleasures of sin for a season.*

This is why so many in the church can sing God's praises, serve in the church, and be good members but refuse to let go of their homosexuality. They enjoy the pleasure of the lifestyle. What's so pleasurable about an abomination, anyway? You must understand that sin has the inherent ability to blind you to its danger and simultaneously fool you with a flood of sensational pleasure. What you may not realize, but will eventually have to face, is that it is ONLY FOR A SEASON. Then, the real fallout begins.

A young man that I had the privilege of ministering to before he passed of AIDS in the year 2000, confessed that very thing to me several days before his death. He had enjoyed his life on the "dl" (down low) in and out of the church, but it had deceived him into a bitter end. I could tell that he had been a very attractive young man, but the disease had robbed him. He was only a pale shadow of what he used to be.

At the urging of my pastor, I went to visit him several days before Christmas. We had a difficult conversation. He recounted his life in the church and his homosexuality. As I sat by his bedside in Atlanta's Piedmont Hospital, he suddenly began pointing at a picture hanging on the wall. "Look!", he exclaimed, "there they are!" I moved closer to him and took his frail hand. It trembled as it clutched mine.

"Minister Foster," he whispered, "I can't say that it was an accident that I got this way. I know what I did. But the others, they better get out before they end up like me." My only response was to squeeze his hand a little tighter. I wished with all of my heart that I could have said a miracle prayer or comforted him in this misery, but it was all in God's hands by that time. Realizing I could have been in the very place he now was, I turned my face away and silently wept. I guess no matter what road we take, we all have to sooner or later, face the consequences of our choices.

My life was not that much different from the young man who lay dying before me. As I looked at him with compassion, God took my mind back to just how good He had been to me in my hour of need.

Walls have a way of forcing you to do things you ordinarily wouldn't consider. Your outlook and state of mind determines if the walls are a tomb or the way to freedom. My walls had one door: suicide. Faced with constant thoughts of killing myself, the simple act of living day to day became a heavy burden. I stopped taking calls from my gay friends and slowed down my nightclub activities. I had dealt with the suicide of my friend Mike, now it was my turn to face the demon. I felt isolated, unprotected and hopeless. I could think of no way out.

I decided that I would show all the people who had hurt me in my life: from my brothers who teased me to the church folks who rejected me. I would show them one, last time that I didn't need them. I would hurt *them* this time. I thought about how my family would cry as they looked at my body. I wanted them to feel very guilty. I planned to leave a letter telling them they were responsible.

In a few days it would be Easter. Easter was a time to celebrate life that Jesus lived which conquered death. I know I had a death wish that only God could stop. That Wednesday before Resurrection Sunday, defeat and desperation embedded itself even deeper into my spirit. I felt my soul slouching into hell. I hated to see the morning sun come through my window. *Why can't I just die in my sleep?* I thought.

The next evening, I came in from work and immediately slumped down in a chair in the living room. I did not want the lights on; the darkness brought an eerie, but welcome aura of being hidden away from my troubles. In the darkness, I fumbled around, found the remote and flipped on the television. At once an amazing scene unfolded before my very eyes. It was as if it was a 3D movie!

There in the scene, a man, beaten and bloodied, drug a heavy wooden cross uphill on a rock-strewn dirt street. Thousands of people lined the street on either side. I noticed the people's faces, all seething with unmasked hate; venomous hate with a murderous intent. This man was the object of their hatred. The hate boiled out and some threw huge stones at him. Some spit at him as he stumbled by. Still, others stretched out their hands and arms, grabbing as if they wanted to rip him apart!

I watched, awed, but yet not comprehending what I saw. Then a question came to my mind. *What did he do to make them hate him so much?* Why were they so angry with him? I had never witnessed such intense hostility in all my days. Though I had been the victim of other's dislike for my lifestyle, this was something that was simply demonic.

Momentarily, I forgot about my own pain as I became engrossed in his dilemma. Suddenly, the man stopped dragging the cross. Everything came to a standstill, frozen as if someone had spoken a magical word. He looked up at me as blood trickled down his face from the thorns pressed into his temples. His tender eyes found mine and I heard his words, audibly and personally: *"I did all of this just for you."* Those eight words signaled a new beginning for me. And then he continued on with his formidable task, carrying the cross to its final destination, on his way to prove his ultimate show of love for me.

LOVE MADE ME BRAND NEW!

This demonstration evoked immediate fear, anticipation and joy in me all at once. I shook uncontrollably and wept shamelessly as the realization of the man's identity swept over me. It was Jesus and at my point of total desperation, he'd found me. The love of Jesus for people like me was richly illustrated in a parable he spoke.

> *Suppose one of you has a hundred sheep and loses one of them. Does he not leave the ninety-nine in the open country and go after the lost sheep until he finds it? And when he finds it, he joyfully puts it on his shoulders and goes home. Luke 15:4 (NIV)*

Indeed, I was lost and Jesus had come to take me home where I belonged. That didn't happen before there was a breaking in my spirit. As I looked into the hateful faces of the crowd, I recognized my own face. A spirit of hate had possessed me for many years. The further I got from God, the stronger the hate became.

The implications of Jesus' eight words struck at soft places in my heart. There was a glimmer of hope for me! I hadn't prayed in over 12 years, and had no clue as to what to say in response or if I should say

119

anything at all. Immediately, the enemy slid next to me and whispered coarsely in my ear: "It's too late. You've done too much and he won't forgive you." I also heard another voice in a soothing tone tell me, "If you ask him, he will forgive you."

I sat in the chair literally quaking with fear, too afraid to ask for fear that I would hear a thunderous voice say "TOO LATE!" But, I was also too afraid to let this chance pass me by. I had been through a lot. I needed peace. I needed Jesus. I got up and went into my back bedroom, the same room I had carried on numerous male sexual affairs, and fell on my face before God. I wanted to say something, but all that I could do was weep over my life of error and rebellion. I struggled for hours, wondering if this was just a fantasy.

I asked God, "How could you love me, after all the evil things I have done?" I named several of the situations I was involved in. He stopped me and with a gentle protest said, "But I love you." I wasn't convinced. Maybe I could shock God and see if He really loved me. Unsure, I recalled a specific incident: "Lord, do you remember when I..." Again He interrupted me and said "But I love you." There was no condemnation in His voice, just the awesome power of forgiveness and mercy. Again, the tears broke anew from my eyes at the prospect of being set free from this prison.

He needed to say nothing more. I repented for my rebellion and sin. I surrendered my life to Him for love's sake and the glory of His presence filled the room. Our fellowship was restored and in a moment, in the twinkling of an eye, He broke the power of sin, including homosexuality over my life! When I rose from the floor, I knew that everything would be all right. A song I had heard so many times growing up now had a vivid meaning to me:

I was sinking deep in sin/Far from the
peaceful shore/Very deeply stained within/
sinking to rise no more/But the master of the
sea, heard my despairing cry/ from the waters
lifted me, now safe am I.
Love lifted me, Love lifted me, when nothing
else could help love lifted me.[9]

The next Sunday, I contacted my friend King and went to church with him. I started attending church regularly and joined with Cathedral of Prayer COGIC. I remained there almost five years, trudging along the long road to healing. I struggled to lay aside the weights and sins that I had grown accustomed to. What did it mean to really be a member of a church? That was something I had never known the extent of, so after joining Cathedral of Prayer, I spent some of the time observing and getting used to being a part of life in the church again. Many of the things I initially saw at Cathedral were not what I was used to growing up.

Amazingly, I still believed that women who wore pants were unsaved. I didn't accept church members playing sports or other activities I felt God didn't approve of. I called home several times to express my displeasure at what I perceived as hypocrisy. This was the residue of my ultra strict upbringing, more the teachings of my church leaders than my mother.

Satan is very devious. I was delivered from homosexuality, but immediately a judgmental spirit took over when I joined the church. I felt justified in it until God said to me, "You will die if you continue to criticize my people." I realized there was still much work the Lord had to do in my life. Salvation was just the door to getting to God. After that, the Holy Ghost rolled up his sleeves to do some serious work on my life and heart.

The process of healing I embarked on included learning how to serve God. I was under a new rule, the rule of love and liberty. I was serving a new Master and He created something wonderful in me. For the first time in my life I knew I was loved, wanted and valued. Since it had been such a long time, I didn't have any idea where I fit into the church structure. I wasn't sure of myself or my ability to even stand up and speak before people. Consequently, I kept silent for some time. But just being at church was not satisfying me. I wanted to do something. I wanted to contribute and show God that I was grateful for Him saving my life.

One Sunday, I came to service dogged by a old feeling that I knew God had taken away from me. In my heart, I wanted to do His will, but I couldn't seem to discover what I should do. In this frame of mind, my desire to serve God was in jeopardy. After the morning service, I stopped Pastor Charles Rodgers on his way out and shared with him my anguish. His tall frame turned slowly to face me.

"I really want to be a part of the church", I said, "but I don't know where I fit in."

Pastor listened patiently and gave me a simple answer: "Well", he said, "whatever your hands find to do, do it with all your might. There's a lot going on around here, so just get yourself involved. I'm sure they would love to have your help."

Pastor's advice was right on target! I jumped in feet first! I joined the choir, the brotherhood, helped out around the church with various projects and assisted the pastor any way that I could. Being actively involved in the life of the church is a vital part of healing.

This may be a good time to discuss the issue of "inclusion." What does inclusion mean for God's church and how far should it go? My circumstances may have turned out different if Pastor Rodgers had reacted negatively towards me. The Lord had instructed me to "tell everyone what I did for you," but I was too afraid of the pastor's rejection if I told him, so I kept quiet. I am not saying he would have rejected me, but I wasn't willing to take the risk to find out. When should you tell your pastor about your past? Is that important? What should the pastor's response be to a member who reveals a homosexual past?

There's a lot of debate going on now concerning just how inclusive pastors should be when it involves *known* homosexual members. Some have argued that since Christ welcomed everyone, homosexuals should be included in every facet of church life. Rev. Jeremiah Wright, pastor of Chicago's Trinity United Church of Christ believes that gays should be.[10] Wright and a growing number of clergy base this belief on the notion that homosexuality isn't sinful.

Others counter that homosexuals should not be a part of the church at all. The infamous Rev. Fred Phelps (God hates fags) of Kansas is well identified with this stance. I believe both perspectives represent extremities that don't represent God. Pastors should apply biblical standards of acceptance equally.

No one should be made to feel unwelcome in the house of God, no matter what sin they are involved in even if they are unrepentant. A KKK member should be as welcome in the house of God as the church mother. If the church is truly a place of healing, then all should be able to come and freely receive God's Word. I understand that there will always be imperfect churches, because there will always be imperfect people in the churches. So banning any type of sinner is just wrong. Coming to church never hurts anyone. Quite the contrary, if the Word is being preached and taught with sincerity, being at church is the best place for a sinner. The problem lies then, with leaders who may be confusing love with authority.

If a person is unrepentant, they shouldn't be allowed into leadership positions within the church. This could signal approval of someone's personal life. At the same time, if a pastor allows adulterers, liars, wife-beaters or otherwise bad vices to be leaders, keeping gays out won't improve the quality of leadership integrity.

16

Off to war!

Cathedral was my second home. I spent more time there than any place. After I had served there for almost a year, war broke out in the Mideast. They called it Operation Desert Shield and my unit, A Company, 197th Support Battalion, 197th Infantry Brigade, was one of the first summoned to go.

War, they say, is hell. Though few of us in the military imagined it at the time, this real war held the potential for many of us coming home in body bags. That was the somber message our captain delivered to us ending weeks of nail biting anxiety. I was attached to the 24th Infantry.

When I received the word that I was to depart 17 days after the conflict started, I had peace about it. My life was in God's hands. And in August 1990, I boarded a ship and took off, a two-week journey over the ocean to a strange land.

The times in the desert were intense: fear, longing,

125

pain and joy. They were all present at one time or another.

None of us could have known how deeply this eight month ordeal would impact our lives both naturally and spiritually. The enemy told me he would make me go back while I was there. "There will be no church, no pastor, no nothing to help you", he threatened. But my faith in God was strong. I knew God was with me, every step of the way and every hour of the day. The Holy Spirit lived in me, helping me to refuse the temptations that came my way.

Yes, the temptations to engage in homosexual acts were real and available, but I was reminded what God had done for me. Letting go of my deliverance meant letting go of my life. Spiritual freedom was more important to me than life itself. Like many soldiers hunkered down in the deserts of Saudi, I experienced times of deep uncertainty brought on by the weeks and weeks of isolation from life back home. Without my spiritual grounding, I would have fallen. The question is would I have gotten up? I didn't want to entertain that thought.

In the face of our Islamic host's adamant refusal to allow any open show of our faith or worship, we formed Bibles studies in our camps. I, along with a Christian female officer whom we called "Mam" and several other brothers and sisters started meeting late at night, after the duty day to sing, study God's Word and pray.

We all approached our desert experience by passionately crying out to God. Not only did God hear our cries, but our fellow soldiers heard them, too! The prayer meetings quickly took root and flourished. Our camp commander was forced to erect a special worship tent to house the standing room only services. We were given special permission to hold a two night revival. We organized a choir and two ministers preached. I saw many saved and others reclaimed their relationship with the Lord.

I remember the letter I wrote home to my mother. "We're in a lot better shape than you think we are," I said. Maybe it had something to do with where we were and the challenge of living each day that made us run to God. I choose to believe that God simply was true to His Word.

> *Then you will call upon me and come and pray to me, and I will listen to you You will seek me and find me when you seek with all your heart (Jeremiah 29:12,13NIV).*

On Easter Sunday, 1991, one year after God changed my life, five members of our prayer group rose early and stood on a sandy hill in Saudi Arabia watching the rising sun come up, a blazing testament to the glory, majesty and goodness of God to us all.

Out in the desert, something churned in my spirit. It was unlike anything I had ever experienced. God was restoring my natural affections. He did it through first giving me a overwhelming desire for children. Back in the states, when I saw fathers holding their children, my heart would ache.

I mentioned earlier that I'd developed an intense dislike of women. Those feelings yielded to feelings of relational insufficiency. Yes, I was a man, but what is a man without someone to carry on his legacy? I was afraid this would happen to me if I was killed during the war. Being a father was a foreign idea to me. It was time to trust God to be the miracle worker I had always heard He was.

One clear night, I took my fears to Him in prayer. The desert air had cooled slightly from the daily 100 degrees we had to battle. I walked out past the tents and trucks to a quiet area. A smooth blanket of sand spread itself out beneath my feet and a bright battalion of stars fell into a watchful formation above. Sensing calm and God's attentive ear I prayed *"Lord, if you will allow me to leave this place alive, I would like to ask you for three sons.*

The sand swallowed up my tears as quickly as they fell. *"Lord, who's going to cry for me if I never get back home? Who will carry on my name?,* I asked. *"What will become of who I am and all the things you have planned for me? But I know that you will be with me to overcome all the fears I have and I trust you in Jesus name."*

The Word of God tells us that anything we ask according to His will, He hears us (1John 5:14). When I finished my prayer, I took out the small Bible I carried and in faith, wrote the names of my three sons. Though it's a bit worn and dirty, I still have that Bible.

I had never been intimate with a woman, and didn't know if I ever would, but within me, the desire to be a father grew stronger and stronger. Thoughts of me holding a child of my own filled my head every night as I prayed.

My faith soared while I was in Saudi Arabia. It may sound a little foolish... well ok, really foolish, but I believed that God purposely arranged the war to get me to a point of faith in Him. We can't minimize the importance of faith in our lives. We need faith for the impossible. We need faith to put the enemy under our feet. Most of all we need faith to please God.

In March 1991, we finally packed up the last truck and took down the last tent and boarded our jet back home.

DON'T ASK, DON'T TELL... JUST FIGHT!

Once a soldier, always a soldier, right? Then from one soldier to another, I want to encourage those of you serving in uniform to trust

God. Although, you are on a physical battle front, be it peacetime or war, your most important battle is the invisible one. Others may not understand the rigors of duty and the pressure to perform placed on you by your willingness to serve our nation. That's enough to cause normal people to crack and run for cover. God will be with you as you reach out to him. It doesn't matter if you're in a foxhole or in a tank, God's Spirit will cover you! He's got your back!

At the core of a soldier's training is the ability to fight and win. Endure hardness as a *good soldier* of Jesus Christ, the Bible tells us. God wants to teach you to fight against what is trying to overcome you. King David, the praiser, was also known for his ability to fight. He declared, "Blessed be the Lord my strength, which teacheth my hands to war and my fingers to fight (Psalms 144:1).

I was never one to run from a fight, even if I knew I couldn't win. When I was in high school, the last big "fight" of my life was with a large, husky girl everyone called "Sugar Mama". Facing Sugar Mama in combat was like facing Goliath. You'd better hope your name was David, and the Lord of Hosts was with you, cause if not you were going to lose.

I'm not sure how she acquired that nickname, but it was far from the truth. Well anyway, silly me in the heat of passion, said a little disparaging remark to Sugar's sister, Loretta about their mama. I should have just committed suicide right then and there! When the word got back to Sugar, she vowed to feed my flesh to the birds after school. Was I scared? Hey, is the Pope Catholic?

The few friends I had, for some reason all decided they were riding home with their parents that day, leaving me alone to face the giantess. Well, to make a long story short, when Sugar finished slinging and smacking me all over the place, I was a mess and couldn't even find one of my shoes. Oh, the joys of high school!

But I still stood and did the best I could. Knowing that in our own weak strength, we could never hope to defeat sexual immorality, we ought to then rely on the power of God to help us fight this thing. You don't have to feel helpless and hopeless, no matter how strong it seems to be in your life. When is the last time you had a good knock down, drag out with the devil over this thing?

If you are struggling with homosexuality and wearing the uniform, don't settle for the military's "don't ask , don't tell" policy. Don't ask, Don't tell is flawed at its core and can only smooth over a social dilemma. It will only deliver a false promise of security. God's policy of ask, seek and knock (Matt 7:7,8) will tell you everything you need to know. Ask Him, and He will give it to you, seek Him and you will find in Him what you need to overcome, knock, and the door of wholeness and deliverance shall be opened unto you. That's God's policy. It's a good one and it never fails.

17
"Will you speak for Me?"

*T*he first time I heard God speak to me, I was deep in the woods of Fort Benning on an FTX (field training exercise) with my military unit. I had never been spoken to in such a direct way by God before so the experience left me quaking with fear.

Throughout the Bible, God spoke to many great men and women: Abraham, Moses, Joshua, Isaiah and Mary the mother of Jesus to name a few. And though we celebrate them now as great men and women of the Bible, in fact they were just ordinary people who had a supernatural encounter with God.

Whoever said God doesn't use ordinary people is just telling a, well...you know what I mean. I wasn't anybody special, I hadn't done anything special, and I didn't know anybody special, yet God came and talked to me.

I was the sergeant of the guard for the fourth shift covering midnight to 3 am. Everyone was weary of the two weeks we had spent training in the field, but as soldiers, this was part of our job. All of it: the field showers, C-rations (later MREs), going to sleep late and getting up early, the stand downs, were part and parcel of being ready. No question about it, we had to be ready to operate under tactical circumstances. I accepted this, that's probably why I had reenlisted for my third tour of duty.

The guard shifts always seemed to come a lot earlier than you wanted them to. But when duty calls, you must answer. So when an unknown arm reached into my tent and shook me, I got up and got dressed. When I got up I went over and woke up my assistant, a young female private named Blige.

It was just a short walk down the dark dirt road to the main position which was manned by a 50 cal machine gun. We completed our initial checks and then settled into our place behind the gun for the next three hours. I was sure it was going to be just as uneventful as all the other numerous times I'd pulled guard. Though we were under a "tactical situation", this was only a peacetime training mission. Still, there were precautions to be taken.

When in the field, soldiers must practice what is known as light and noise discipline. Light and noise discipline requires that soldiers refrain from displaying any forms of light including fires or engage in any conversations or activities which give off the unit's position to the enemy. It is a purely defensive precaution, because the unit is in stand down or the majority are at rest for the night. The guards, because they are the primary watchmen for the unit, are charged with ensuring this regimen is enforced.

Blige and I staked out our spots in the hole and I began to peer out into the darkness. This was futile because it was pitch black and there were no discernible landmarks except the trees in the distance. I always tried to take my watch duty seriously, simply because it was serious duty. The lives of my fellow soldiers depended on my vigilance. Blige promptly plopped back into the hole and went to sleep.

When I heard her snoring softly, I thought to myself *see, that's why I don't like working with female soldiers.* But I didn't wake her. It was better for me (though I could have gotten in trouble) to let her sleep.

About 45 minutes into our shift, a loud voice shattered the silence and caused me to leap to my feet!

"Darryl!", the voice called out urgently.

The suddenness of this "attack" made my mind reel, churning to understand exactly *who* was calling me and *why?* Why at this time? Everybody in the field knew that we were under light and noise discipline. I fully expected my platoon sergeant to come hustling down the path to jump all over me. The other perplexing component to this was the use of my first name. In the military (especially among enlisted soldiers) it's customary to address each other by last name when on duty. That is, unless you are personal friends.

But this voice, called me distinctively by my first name and did it quite loudly.

My next inclination was to check with Blige, the sleeping female soldier, to see if she too had been startled by this intrusion of the field silence. When I turned and shook her she mumbled "hunnnn?" That answered my question. Now, I was really scared.

With all of the possibilities of a natural explanation explored and still no answer, I was simply perplexed. And still I saw no one and heard no one approach me. Then as quickly as it had come before, the voice rushed in again.

"Darryl!"

The hair on my arm "stood up" and I felt the goose pimples rise all along my skin. Trembling, I began to realize something out of the ordinary was happening. In my mind, I saw a quick vision of the boy Samuel and God calling his name. *So this is what this is,* I said in my mind! *God is calling me.* Surprising enough, the call came a third time and the sense of urgency was clear.

"Darryl!"

And this time, I responded to the voice of God.

"If it's you Lord, speak to me and I will listen." I said softly.

"Don't turn to the right, neither the left", the voice warned, "but keep straight ahead."

I was saved and filled with the Holy Spirit and both my father and grandfather were preachers, but the dots never connected in my head. I never guessed in a million years what God was really saying to me. It would be several months later before that realization became clear in my heart.

"Go and stand up behind the pulpit!", commanded Mother Carol McGruder. She was almost 6 feet tall and looked at me like a mother demanding something from a reluctant son. I was very reluctant. What could God possibly want with me? The more I tried to force His call from my mind, the stronger it was when it returned. I could not conceive that I could be someone who would dare speak for God. I thought that my life had to be 100% perfect and that was light years away. I had a lot of work to do on myself and I knew that God wasn't finished with me either, but here I was.

"Go!" she commanded again.

It was Wednesday night Bible study, but it had turned into a midweek revival service. I had just witnessed my best friend Kelly give his life to the Lord. The saints at church that night were reeling from the anointing in the room. That's when the attention turned on me. I heard Mother McGruder's voice for sure, but my body refused to obey.

I looked around, hoping maybe the pastor would stop it, but he looked at me as if to say, "I can't help you man."

I began to weep, realizing something I did not want to happen was fast closing in on me, ready to change my life again, ready to take me into something with completely new challenges. Was I ready for that? Finally, I walked up the steps into the pulpit and stood there. Mother McGruder promptly made her pronouncement: "That's where you belong said the Lord!"

It wasn't until three months later, in February that I accepted what God and his "cloud of witnesses" told me. He pursed me relentlessly until in an odd way, under my bed, I relented and said yes. God called me to preach and teach His word. Before, I was petrified as I heard Him ask me the "question" *Will you speak for me?* I thought that I was the least likeliest candidate to be a preacher. I felt I was not qualified in any sense and couldn't imagine why God would want me.

Is God calling other exhomosexuals? Yes, I believe He is. He called Pastor Donnie McClurkin (read his book "Eternal Victim/Eternal Victor!"). Down in Miami, He called Miriam Passmore out of 20 years as a lesbian, "stud" and "drag king" performer. God called worship leader and songwriter Dennis Jernigan who now fathers 9 children. He called Chris Johnson, Sr. out of the lifestyle and even with HIV, God blessed him wife a beautiful wife and three wonderful children. These men and women, along with many others, are in ministry to meet the needs of brothers and sisters who are falling through the religious cracks.

Being in ministry is all about meeting the needs. My former pastor, Dr. Gilbert Gillum, Jr. cultivated that ministry philosophy in me. He always said "find the need and meet the need." Maybe without knowing it, he imparted a powerful truth to me.

In his office, Pastor Gillum had just finished listening to my litany of complaints about homosexuality in the church.

"Somebody needs to do something, pastor." I said.

He looked me in the eye and said, "You're somebody. You do something."

He was right. God has equipped all of us to make a difference. The only thing stopping us is us.

The harvest is plentiful, but the laborers are few. If you look around you, you will undoubtedly see many people who need deliverance. They need to know what God can do and they need a friend who understands what they are going through. That's why God is calling us up and leading us out. The church has tended to be insensitive to people in homosexual sin, but God will hear their cries for freedom and send someone to deliver them.

> *The Lord said, I have indeed seen the misery of my people in Egypt, I have heard them crying out because of their slave driver and I am concerned about their suffering, so I am come down to rescue them Exodus 3:7,8 (NIV).*

He did it before and He will do it again! Deliverance is His job!

18
Real restoration takes time

or everything real, there is a false counterpart. Real restoration takes time, effort and perseverance. It takes diligence and it takes commitment. Anything worthwhile is worth fighting for. Don't settle for the false counterpart to restorative healing from homosexuality. Don't be seduced by shortcuts and easy outs. In the long run, you'll find yourself back at square one.

What does real restoration mean? To restore means to bring back to the original condition of usefulness. God wants to bring you back to your original condition of holiness. We were created holy. That's God's original intent and Adam's original state before the fall.

> According as he hath chosen us in him before
> the foundation of the world, that we should be
> holy and without blame before him in love
> (Ephesians 1:4).

Holiness is our goal, our mark and our passion. That

is only achieved as you "run the race with patience that is set before you." (Hebrews 12:1). Everyone has a race to run and a road to run it on. Speed is not the issue, endurance is.

The road to healing from homosexuality can be long and complicated by the stumbling blocks placed in your way by other believers. Many brothers and sisters do not make it. They are simply starved to death of spiritual love, fellowship and mentoring by the church. They return to the world, or to a false religion convinced that they could not change. Thank God that even through my trials and tribulations, I could always hear God's personal message to me, "But, I love you."

In my race to maturity, many "issues" had to be addressed. "issues" are those peripheral abstracts in your life. You must root them out, hunt them down and then systematically destroy them one by one. Issues are what you never testify about in church, you just dance when you've destroyed one. If somebody in church asks you what's going on, just do a little Holy Ghost hop and say "Another one bites the dust!"

After 11 years saturated by immorality, the Holy Spirit showed me how to live holy and how to possess my body in sanctification and honor. The first year I was saved I "fell" sexually several times. As the guilt and shame of my actions haunted me, I searched for the reasons I would violate my covenant.

I could blame it on the fact that I knew nothing about support groups. I could have excused it by saying there was no one to talk to. I had no role models or websites or help lines. I could have easily slid into that mindset and killed my deliverance. I felt "I was doing all I knew to do", but God let me know there was some things in my life I needed to let go of. If healing cannot be proactive in your life, then it is worthless. Besides my struggle with going to nightclubs, another stronghold was the sense of being alone and the sadness it brought. Here I was: no friends, and far away from my family. I had not yet bonded with my church family. What's a single young brother to do when those "moments" come on him?

Let's talk about loneliness and those feelings you and I struggle against from time to time. I believe many people, whether homosexual or not, battle with this unseen, elusive foe. All of us have felt its sting, but maybe none as pronounced as Jesus on the cross. "My God, My God why hast thou forsaken me?," he cried out to the Father. No one wants to feel abandoned or unwanted. So while the need is a legitimate one, a lack of understanding about that need, leads to it controlling you, instead of you controlling it.

Alfonzo Surrett, a former manager and singer with the gospel group Commissioned said in one magazine article many homosexual men had confided in him that "loneliness is a major force that pushed them into homosexual relationships."[11] He added that one of their greatest fears was rejection by other men.

Loneliness is a spirit that struggles and resists the presence of God in your life. Loneliness gives you a false reading of your life with Christ, causing you to think that He is not with you. It assaults your mind like a contagious disease. What that does is force you to seek other ways to fulfill this need for companionship. Remember, that's what the sex used to accomplish? But now we have a new friend, one that will stick closer than a brother.

Jesus said that he would never leave us nor forsake us; that he would be with us always even until the end of the earth. What does that mean to you and do you believe his promise? I did, but only in my head, instead in my heart. What's the answer for a lonely heart? I believe it's God's peace. Just like faith and fear don't mix, loneliness and peace cannot co-exist. Look at this wonderful verse:

> *Thou wilt keep him in perfect peace*
> *whose mind is stayed on thee, because he*
> *trusteth in thee* (Isaiah 26:3).

You can never go wrong when you trust God. Trusting Him erases the fear of going forward in your life. Remember the steps of a good man are ORDERED by the Lord.

What are you really saying when you allow loneliness to push you back into a sexual situation? You're saying "God, I don't believe you are Emmanuel, I don't believe you are with me." Is that what you really believe? If He is with you, then you are never alone. If you confess that, the peace of God that passes all understanding will be with you and give you comfort, even in the midst of raging storms.

The Holy Spirit showed that each time I fell sexually, I was demonstrating that I did not believe God was with me. Each time I fell, I was seeking to fig leaf my loneliness with what had been familiar to me. And for me, that was sex with another male.

I discovered I had to give my lonely heart to the Lord and patiently cry out to him for complete assurance. As I sought to be closer to Him, the attractions of other men slowly began to subside. I realized that the more of Jesus Christ I allowed to fill my heart, soul, and mind, the less I wanted to seek anything outside of his will for me. We have to be completely sure that Christ lives in us (1 Corinthians 13:5).

We should never, ever make excuses for our sin. That is a spiritually fatal mistake. The moment you justify any wrong you've done, satan is able to access your life and set up camp in that area.

I knew that I was saved, but an unresolved anger at my father remained. Along with the sexual dysfunction, anger had controlled and manipulated much of my life. It didn't go away in a poof of smoke. The deep wounds needed the soothing balm of the Word to heal them.

That's why I went to church often. I needed to hear the Word. By letting it mend me and reveal my deficiencies, I could be sure I was taking steps to success. We have to allow the Word of God to actively confront error in us. Make no mistake about it, the past isn't quite dead, so the flesh must be trained not to react.

UNDERSTANDING THE PROCESS OF HEALING

Bear with me as I say this. I have been out of the homosexual lifestyle for almost 12 years now, and I am not yet healed. I am not yet completely healed from the sinful wounds I suffered during the 11 years as an active adult homosexual and the 5 or 6 years I struggled with the "feelings of my infirmities". I am, without question, not the man I used to be, but I am far from being the man of God I was created to be. No excuses here, just a process every believer must go through on the road to full maturity in Christ.

> *Till we all come in the unity of faith, and of the knowledge of the Son of God, unto a perfect man, unto the measure of stature of the fullness of Christ: that we henceforth no more be children, tossed to and fro, and carried about with every wind and doctrine, by the sleight of men, and cunning craftiness, whereby they lie in wait to deceive." (Ephesians 4:13,14)*

It is the misunderstanding of perfection[12] (relative maturity) and perfectionism (absolute holiness) that has hindered true recovery and restoration of not only former homosexuals, many types of "ex" sinners in the church. A 2 year old must grow and mature by the natural course of living, therefore you cannot expect him or her to think or act as you would someone who is 20 years of age.

In Joel 2:25, God promises to "restore all the years that the cankerworm hath eaten away". In other words, God promises to bring back things the enemy had stolen. We can never put God on a time table. He moves according to His own sovereign will. So it requires patience to let God complete His work in us.

To some people my claim that I am not yet completely healed from homosexuality may conjure up images of continued secret sexual encounters, but that is far from being true. I am simply living in the time of recovery, submitting myself to God to flush, clean out and rebuild the waste places in my life.

If you and I submit ourselves to God for divine inner healing of our souls, we could experience a deeper intimacy with Him and a greater sense of His presence in us as we worship. But if we settle for the "microwave mentality" of our generation, it will push us to act and feel as if God doesn't know what He's doing. Our timetable says He should be finished in a few weeks or a few months or even a few years. If He isn't, then what will you do? Take matters into your own hands?

I'm so glad, as the song says, that man didn't make me. People, unlike God, can be impatient and critical of you when you are in the healing process and they cannot understand it. This is one of the reasons we see so many people stumbling back into their homosexual sins. They have been rushed out of the hospital by impatient church "doctors" who are tired of helping them.

The time frame for healing is as varied as there are individual people. Dr. Gloria Johnson Rodgers, my former first lady, said the physical healing of the body or the amount of recovery time of a wounded body is dependent on two things. First, the procedure used to treat the wound and secondly, if the person has other diseases in the body.

For example, a diabetic's healing process is usually slower, because the individual's body simply does not have all the natural resources in place to speed up the healing. There is no magic shot or pill the diabetic can take, it is just a simple fact of time and patience with the process. On the other hand, Dr. Rodgers said, "Places in the body with increase vasculature (blood vessels) like the face, scalp and head area heal extremely fast. Stitches in these areas usually come out in three days versus the rest of the body which may take 5-7 days."

Now, I'm not a doctor and I have never studied medicine, but it's clear that the process of healing the body takes, with all of its circumstances and particulars, is astonishingly parallel to the spiritual process of healing. The sooner we come to understand this, the sooner we will begin to experience what it means to "be made whole."

Four years ago, my mother's health began rapidly deteriorating. At first, we thought that it was just a passing illness. But we became alarmed when her weight continued to plummet and she lost her appetite. My mother doesn't believe in going to the doctors, because that is what she was taught. It took a lot of prayer and crying to convince her to finally go and get it checked out. I was shaken, because I love her so much and did not want to face losing her then. We prayed and anointed her body, asking God for a miracle.

The physician who examined her, took several tests and two days later, called us and instructed us to get her to the hospital immediately for surgery. Mother was diagnosed with colon cancer which caused her to progressively lose several pints of blood through her bowels.

The situation was critical! Had she gone a few more days in this condition, he said she would have died.

Praise God, the emergency operation was a success! The immediate threat was removed, thereby saving her life. But that was only the beginning. She spent five days in the hospital just for initial recovery. The first two days, she could not speak. She barely opened her eyes. She was fed liquids.

I sat by her bedside watching and praying, but the process of recovery could go no faster than the healing would allow. On the third day, the nurses insisted she began moving around. Although it caused her great pain, she began moving so that her blood could circulate. It was painful, but necessary.

Little by little she regained her strength, but even upon discharge we learned that it would be several months before she was completely healed. During that time she was given weekly low radiation chemo shots. It took time, patience, love and understanding, but I have a healthy mother today.

The lessons that will get us to maturity are abundant, if we will take heed. There's no need to rush recovery if you want true, lasting healing from homosexuality.

Trials bring maturity which in turn teaches you patience and endurance. And maturity gives you the strength to step forward even further for the more difficult challenges that lie ahead. I know how Esther must have felt in the critical hour she was called upon to save her people. There was great fear, but she decided it was worth risking death to save them.

Likewise, through the test of trials, I am willing to risk it all to let the truth be known about homosexuality in order to save anyone who will listen. Yes, I believe God has brought us for such a time as this.

He has never been without a witness to His power. It's not about us, but about Him.

He will always show Himself strong. He did it on Mt. Carmel in a powerful show of fire. And He's doing it for us who are standing up in our churches and communities to proclaim that God does indeed change homosexual sinners.

I've learned to believe God with radical faith. Nothing He has promised me shall be denied in my time and season. I've learned that trouble, affliction and sorrow is the lot for every saint, but the joy comes in knowing that God will deliver you out of them all. What a mighty God we serve! I've learned in my struggle to overcome homosexuality, that I must deny my flesh its "rights" under the Adamic law and release my spirit man into freedom under the new covenant with Christ.

With all of the negativity and doubt directed at exhomosexuals, healing itself can become a radical experience. Healing is never easy for anyone who has been ravaged by sin, but it is a necessary and critical element if you or I want to recover from homosexuality. This is where the gay rights movement stumbles and is confused. Activists gauge change by logical human standards instead of the reliability of God's Word. *He sent His word and healed them* (Psalms 107:20).

Gay activists believe that if you say you are changed, then to prove it, you must show them evidence of never having another struggle. They believe that temptation equals sin. If that were true, then Jesus, completely failed even before he started. He was *led by the Spirit* to be tempted (Mark 1:12:13). The Bible never promises any such sort of spiritual utopia for believers. The scripture even tells us that in the face of ANY temptation, which are common (homosexuality included) that God has, with the temptation, provided a way of escape.

We all must continue to struggle against the will of the flesh and cast down vain imaginations, knowing that one day full redemption is coming. The carnal man cannot understand the things of the Spirit, because they are spiritually discerned. The reason there is a rise in homosexual affirming theology is because folks are in the flesh.

Some use the example of Paul's "thorn in the flesh" to justify acceptance of their homosexuality. But Paul did not accept his thorn, he accepted God's grace. It's very clear that, whatever that thing was, he wanted it gone! The question should not be CAN HOMOSEXUALS CHANGE (focus on people), the question should be CAN GOD CHANGE HOMOSEXUALS (focus on God)? We must continue to declare change happens, according to the word of faith. *And such were some of you* (1 Corinthians 6:11).

Satan will do everything within his power to destroy your progress towards freedom. He is a slave master who hates that his "property" is gone. He will work through anyone that will let him, regardless of the label hanging around their necks. I had to realize this early in my walk. Satan did not want me to make it. The demonic forces that had held me for many years were in a rage that Christ had set me free. Being spiritual is one thing, but restoration also means getting to the practical side of your life.

BREAKING FREE: LEARNING TO LIVE PRACTICAL HOLINESS

I strongly advise you to embrace practical holiness as a tool of overcoming sexual struggles in your life. Practicality speaks to the application (doing) of wisdom. In other words, what you know, then you must do. Even after I received God's Spirit into my life, worshipped and praised God, read my Bible and prayed, I still needed to **live** Monday, Tuesday, Wednesday, Thursday, Friday and Saturday.

I have seen way too many people who quote scripture after scripture yet seem to have no power being produced in their lives. There is just no fruit of what they say. I found out that you must mix faith (quoting scriptures and hearing the gospel) with action. What you believe, you must do. James taught that principle in Chapter 2, verse 14. It is good to get the Word in your heart, but you must also let the Word *work* in your heart to affect your life in a real way.

I remember when my hanging buddy Greg, called me the next week after I had given my life to Christ. He wanted to know where I had been.

"I ain't seen you, what you been into?, he asked. He got ready for one of those sensational stories I was famous for after the weekends. Greg was always the melodramatic type.

I didn't skip a beat. "I got me a new man!" I said.

"Oh my God, Darryl!", he exclaimed, "where did you scoop him up from? I knew you hadn't been out (to the club) cause you been sneaking around!"

"No, man it's not like that, this man is special and changed my life. I gave my life to the Lord and I don't want to do all those things I used to do," I explained.

"Oh, (long pause) that's nice." he said, a little deflated. Greg called me several more times before he finally realized I didn't want to get back into that lifestyle.

Living for Christ requires that we strike a balance between the spiritual and the natural. The Bible explains in 1 Corinthians 15:46, that the "spiritual did not come first, but the natural and after that the spiritual" (NIV). In other words, even after God saves us from our homosexuality and all of the paraphernalia of that lifestyle, we cannot

147

go into hiding. We can't stick our heads in the sand and hope that we never have to face trials, temptations and failures. The only place that happens is in the Looking Glass with Alice in Wonderland. Life after homosexuality goes on! Doing that requires taking stock of what has affected us and what is familiar to us as tokens of our past life in sin. We have to start — right away — identifying things, people and places that will stand in the way of our quest for freedom.

In Joshua 7:13 God said that Isreal would not achieve victory over their enemies until they removed the things that were bringing a curse upon them. I was led by the Holy Ghost to get rid of the "idols" of my past, whatever they were. A literal house cleaning. God didn't tell me to pray about the situation, He said to throw those things out. To set specific rules to rid myself of some things that could cause me immediate danger. I want to share some things that I did to solidify my deliverance.

1. *Get rid of anything in your immediate surroundings that remind you of your past life.*

Throw it out! I had a weakness for "deep-house" Chicago-style club remixes, (some of you know what that is). If I listened to it, incredibly, my mind would wander to certain situations (sexual or otherwise) that had occurred when the song was playing. Music and memory combine to create a powerful stumbling block to your freedom. The mind possesses the incredible ability to retain vivid images of past events that it can call up in a moment's notice. Music is a powerful mechanism that facilitates this. Getting rid of risky items includes magazines of men or women. Even if they are not sexually explicit, they can cause your mind to stretch its imagination beyond what it should. As Jesus said, this is "tempting the Lord thy God."

2. *Change your travel patterns when out so that you don't go by places that offer sexually explicit materials.*

Videos and nude magazines cannot walk or drive a car, so if you do not bring them home they will not be there. Cut off all physical sources. Pornography is hypnotic and extremely seductive. The closer you get to it, the more alluring it becomes. In other words, do what is in your power to resist the pull into it. This is a wise saying: Out of sight, out of mind.

3. *Get involved in a church that teaches and lives the Bible.*

I did. I realize that no church is perfect, but the choice of where you worship can mean the difference in you falling back into sin or standing strong in Christ. Avoid places where other homosexuals attend, but seem not to want to change, that is an indication that the gospel is not being preached in its purest form. Churches have many "service" ministries that you can involve yourself in. I did everything from picking up paper to singing in the choir to cleaning bathrooms. You think humility doesn't get God's attention? Try it! Serve others and God will lift you up above those things that are trying to keep you down.

4. *Deal with the underlying, root issues that cause you to do what you do.*

As I dealt with my issues of loneliness, I began to see more clearly that I used it as a excuse to fall into sexual temptations. That led me back to what was "familiar" to me: sex with men. Thank God it only happened a few times after I was free, but it was critical I recognized that "spirit" and avoided letting it rule me. How? Sometimes, I put on a favorite praise and worship CD and cried out for God to love me. Sometimes, I called my friend and just talked with them about my desire to be holy and right before God. Sometimes, I read the Bible

149

and deeply contemplated on its meaning to my life. Whatever you can do, break the "hands" that keep pulling at you to return to what you used to do. Getting enrolled in a holistic healing course like Living Waters, offered by local Exodus International ministries or Lifelines, our ministry's 6 month discipleship program (see online resources at the end of the book). Both can be very helpful.

5. *BE ACCOUNTABLE to someone in authority if possible.*

The lack of accountability is another big cause of people returning to the lifestyle. However, one of the hurdles is finding someone to trust with your faults. We still live among "church folk" who operate in ignorance and mistrust, yet Godly accountability (James 5:16) will keep you out of many things, that could otherwise pull you away from God. Confide in someone you totally trust, but is REMOVED from being any part of enticement into sin. This someone should be understanding of your situation and not be "surprised" if you have to confess a sinful act or thought to them. Does such a person exist? Yes, they are out there somewhere. Ask God to show you who it is.

6. *Watch out for doubletalk.*

Lifestyle doubletalk is quicksand to an overcomer. By that, I mean, people may speak one thing but you know and they know it has a sexual subtext to it. I've found out that this comes from church folk as frequently as it comes from someone in the "world". Doubletalk entraps your mind and creates a hunger to fulfill any sexual desires that arise out of it. Stop late night phone calls from guys talking in their "bedroom" voice. For you sisters, you know when that other sister has something other than going higher in the Lord on her mind. When the Spirit speaks that to you, be wise and bow out of the conversation.

I realize you may not want to hurt the other person's "feelings", but you have got to make some hard choices. Hurt feelings may have to happen, if that person is unwilling to respect your decision to break free.

It's a good idea not to receive calls other than from family members after 10 pm. That's right, set some standards in your life and take charge. Stop letters, emails, "instant messages" or meetings with any man or woman (if you struggle with lesbian desires), who is not helping you to be successful in your walk. It may sound like a lonely road, but to save your life it becomes necessary to cut excess from it.

7. Be honest with God.

God is someone you simply cannot fool. Honesty with the Father helped pull me through some of my most heated battles with male lust. Tell it to Him like it is and ask His help to overcome it. And then move on. Jesus Christ truly understands what you are going through and knows how to help you. Read Hebrews 4:15 and 1 Corinthians 10:12-14. Honesty should never be the best policy, it should be your *only* policy.

19
Finding Ms "Good Thing"

I found out that getting married is a scary thing. Especially when you're a man who has spent almost half of his life developing same gender feelings and sexual attractions.

Two years after I had left homosexual living, joined Cathedral of Prayer and began to develop in my walk with the Lord, I met a beautiful young lady, Dee, whom I later developed a strong attraction to.

Green tree leaves were reluctantly turning into golden browns and reds as summer handed over the keys to fall. That was when I first saw her. I was on my way to choir rehearsal at church after a night of pulling 24 hour duty at the barracks. I was about to pull up to the stop light right by Friendship Baptist Church in Columbus when I saw her hurriedly walking up the steps of the church. Dee was absolutely beautiful! She was adorned in a long red coat, a perfect piece in the season colorful mosaic. I thought about the possibility of meeting her for a second and then said to myself...nawwww. Little did I know it was a moment of destiny. A few minutes later, as I stood in front of Cathedral talking to (actually getting reprimanded by) Pastor Rodgers, she drove up, got out and asked if we were having service. I had no idea why she was looking for church service on a Saturday morning. We talked briefly and I invited her back to service the next day.

The Lord works in mysterious ways! My best friend Kelly Poree and I always sat in the choir stands together right behind the pastor. That Sunday I sat behind Kelly. When "Ms Dee" walked in church, she looked like a movie star! She had on those rose colored glasses and that long, sexy red coat. Kelly turned around and gave me the eye. We both smiled.

I later found out that Kelly's wife Charlotta was furious with him! She told us that in a "nightmare" she saw a pretty young woman come to church and her husband was flirting with her. I guess you can figure out that Dee's entrance set it off. Charlotta thought Kelly was smiling at Dee and her nightmare was coming true! Thank God we were able to explain it all to her! We all laughed about it after Dee and I married.

Dee and I didn't date right off, because I was, quite honestly, not secure in my masculinity or how to approach a woman. I had resigned myself to meeting a goal of lifelong celibacy. Satan constantly attacked my mind about my desire to be married. His standard line was "you won't know what to do with a woman." Even though I was very hesitant at first to pursue a relationship with a woman, something about Dee stood out in a special way. The wife of a friend said to me once, "it takes a special kind of woman to be married to you men." I agree, Dee was very special.

In August 1992, I landed a job working for American Airlines, which required me to train in Dallas for about two months. During that time our interest in each other blossomed. She wrote addressing me as "Minister Foster" in her letters. She was always sweet and respectful. And I liked that a lot. I may not have known a lot about women, but I knew that I didn't want a pushy, controlling woman.

I like to think that I decided to love her, instead of falling in love with her. I decided that I wanted to spend my life with this woman.

I was very blessed to have a friend in my life like Kelly. He's one guy that I love with all my heart. He has been my "thick and thin" friend for over 12 years now. I credit him for letting God use him and his wife to bring about my eventual marriage to Dee. What did he do?

Well, for one, Kelly always encouraged me to take advantage of the signals coming Dee. If I seemed hesitant about talking to Dee, He encouraged me by saying "Man, she really likes you!" or "I think you and her would make a good couple." He and his wife even invited me over one night for dinner, but didn't tell me Dee had baked the chocolate cake I was wolfing down with delight! Thank God for friends like them! Matchmakers!

When I returned from training with my new job in September 1992, I was ready to ask Dee to be my wife! Yes, the time had arrived. I was about to cross over an important threshold in my life. I decided from the very beginning that I would not hide my past from her. I think being honest and upfront is the very best option for exgay men considering marriage. A prospective mate should be given the decency and respect to choose if she will accept you. Concealing it, even if you are afraid, is dishonest and will cause serious trust problems later on in the marriage. I have seen too many marriages involving these circumstances fall apart as the secrets of the past come creeping in.

I didn't know what Dee's response would be to my confession, but

I knew that I had to tell her. I called her to ask if I could come by and see her later that night. I had already purchased the engagement ring and went to her apartment. Don't worry, we were very respectful of each other. We were both saved. Well, all I can say is that I made it through my proposal, bumbling, sweating, (even through my confession) to hear her say YES!

What happened next is all a haze, but I do remember running out of the door screaming SHE SAID YES!! SHE SAID YES! at the top of my lungs. It was about 11:30 at night and I'm sure I woke some folks up with my excitement. That began our life together.. We were married on October 24, 1992 in a beautiful service at Cathedral. We will always be thankful to our Cathedral family, especially the late Mrs. Gwendolyn Wilkes who was a great blessing to Dee and I.

FAVOR AND ARROWS

The second part of Proverbs 18:22 is the real revelation of what a wife is to her husband. A man who marries a good woman is all but guaranteed to get favor from the Lord. I always say God did me a big favor by giving me a wife. I still hold true to my old school teaching that a man needs to search for his wife. She is out there, hidden like a box of valuable jewels. Some men make the mistake of waiting for their wife to come to them, when they should be out looking. If you want her brothers, get out there and start looking!

I don't mean to be insensitive, cause I'm married now, but I'm trying to help brothers, especially like me who lacked the confidence to be aggressive in the search for your "piece of favor." That's why it's very important to form relationships with other Christian men who have not experienced homosexuality. They have some insight and wisdom that you need to seek and find a woman that's right for you.

God has blessed us with children. My "quiver" filled up pretty quick! Brittanie was 3 years old when I married her mother. Then, Philip Aaron Micheal came along in August 1993 and Charlie, who we named after the founder of the COGIC, Bishop C.H. Mason, joined us in December 1994 (I know, kind of close!) and our little darling and sweetheart (and family boss), Trinity Gabrielle joined our family on Super Bowl Sunday, 1999! We decided to name her after everyone in heaven. They are the answers to the prayers I prayed out in the desert.

The joy my wife and children have given me is unspeakable and full of glory. It was a special miracle and a slap in the devil's face, for me, a man who used to hate women, to now be a father and a husband. Again, I believe this was another plank in the bridge to healing. My wife and children were and are pivotal keys to me finding my place as a man and more importantly, as a man of God.

As I said before, Charlie and Philip had come into my life. Two precious sons of my own. The Holy Spirit said to me, "You must find your father and forgive him, or you will never have a right relationship with your sons." I instantly knew what he meant and I did not want those curses of broken family relations to haunt me and my sons.

I began asking questions beginning with my mother and then with another woman he'd had a brief relationship with. So I set about looking for him and quickly found him. I talked with my father briefly on the phone and told him that I was bringing my boys by to see him. That next Sunday, we all went to visit him. He was very glad to see me, my wife and children. I forgave him. I didn't ask him anything about why he left us. I just sat there and enjoyed being with my daddy.

My sons seem genuinely puzzled to know that I had a daddy. They asked me all sorts of questions like "did my dad ever spank me? Did my dad take me to the store? I told them that I hadn't seen my dad in a long time, but we would make up for it. During our visit, my Dad told Philip that I was a happy baby. "Darryl always laughed and played with his little striped ball," he said. A wave of emotion went through my heart. He put a valuable piece of my missing life together. It helped tremendously in overcoming my anger and feelings of abandonment.

IS MARRIAGE FOR YOU?

Some people think that when a man who has a homosexual past gets married it is just an attempt to run away the troubles that used to plague him. I remember talking to a church brother (who was on the dl) about his homosexuality. He indicated to me that he was the type that only went for married men. He knew that I was married and had children, but acted unconcerned.

"Hummmph!, he snorted at me, "I know plenty of married men who are still messing around." He probably was telling the truth, but that's not a blanket condemnation of all of us who choose marriage.

From my understanding, marriage is a good thing, but can be fraught with problems. God created the blueprint for the union of male and female. Despite what the shrill voices of those who advocate for so-called "homosexual unions" or gay marriages" say, only the creator can order His blueprint be changed. So far, according to the scriptures I have read and studied (over 25 passages in all) none of them even remotely convey that God has changed his original intent: One (biological) man with one (biological) woman for life (Gen 1:27). Sorry, due to the times, I had to qualify that statement.

The biggest problem with people and marriage, even from the times of Moses, is that people are too quick to see God through their failures. Jesus said that Moses allowed divorce, not because it was God's will, but because of the hardness of their hearts (Matthew 19:8). God sets the standards and we should reach for them. Paul called it pressing towards the mark. Instead, in the case with marriage, we fail to meet God's standards so often we begin believing that *our* way (divorce) is the way it should be. Not true. Of course, I'm not at all suggesting that divorce is an unforgivable sin, just that God's STANDARD never changes.

Having said that, I ask the question for all you brothers out there desiring to marry and father children, is it for you? I firmly believe that a man who finds a wife, finds a good thing. However, we must understand that sexual brokenness is a sad fact of man's fallen nature. Men who marry women without being solidly on the road to healing from that brokenness, are asking for trouble once they enter into the relationship. I always advise brothers who call me, to first talk with their pastor and to get premarital counseling, and I think that is always good advice.

I did not discuss my homosexual past with my first pastor and that was a mistake. Not getting that off my chest caused me a lot of pain later with my wife. This usually rotated around my feeling that Dee did not "understand" my bouts with temptation. Of course, she didn't because I never talked to her about it. Neither did I talk to my pastor. It was a trap. Later, after we moved to Texas things got progressively worse between us. Without any role models for our type of marriage and my strong hesitancy to discuss my past with anyone, we were left to fend for ourselves in solving marital problems.

That does not have to happen today. There are a lot more

resources and couples (Dee and I for one) who are willing to discuss these types of things for the benefit of couples facing the same situations we faced. Marriage for the exhomosexual man or woman should be **their decision and their decision only.** You should never allow anyone, including spiritual leaders, to force you into marriage if you know you're not ready for it. Sometimes, people enter marriage with false expectations. They think that it will just run off of love fumes for the rest of their days, but that's not necessarily true.

Remember, Marriage is like a car. Love is like the wheels, but commitment is the gas. You can have the best set of wheels on your car that money can buy, but without gas in the tank, they will never perform their most basic function. Committing to stay together is what keeps you going through the misunderstandings, errors, trials and valleys. Those vows say "for better or worse, richer or poorer, in sickness and in health." That's what marriage is: knowing that you will be faced with your fair share of troubles, but understanding that love and patience and Jesus will see you through every one of them. This is fundamental to all marriages.

It is impossible to tell every man with a homosexual past if marriage is the best thing for him or if it is an option at all (I'll let one of the women write a book to talk to the sisters). But for me it was the best thing that happened to me. My wife and I are yet developing respect for each other, realizing that we both had great difficulties to overcome as we became one. Because we both chose to trust Christ as the heart of our marriage, we've endured hard storms many other couples like us haven't lasted through.

My wife has been the untold story of success in living out my deliverance. She was instrumental in encouraging me to begin sharing my story, even when I had serious reservations about it. I just wanted to be a good little COGIC preacher and forget all about what I had been through, but God had other plans for me.

She always urged me to be obedient to God so that others could hear and be free. I guess that's why David said in Psalm 32:2, "My soul shall make her boast in the Lord: the humble shall hear thereof and be glad." She and I both share our testimony openly to give courage to other couples who are struggling with these issues.

Many times when I was angry or frustrated about the call of God on my life, she was there to encourage me, telling me that God didn't create me to fail. While I do not know if marriage is an must for all ex-homosexuals, I know that for me, it was God's way of showing His love and desire for me to be made whole.

Since Dee and I have made our lives as public as we can, we have come to know many wonderful married couples who, like us, are reaching to enrich our lives through submission to Christ and loving one another and our children. They may not all be as openly aggressive as we are about "exgay" ministry, but all of them know that God is more powerful than any situation they face. I believe if called upon they'll testify to that.

Not every marriage is going to last out till "death do us part". So many women who have been married to homosexual men who have returned to the lifestyle feel as though they are consigned to a tomb of silent suffering. But it does not have to be so. A woman is a precious jewel who has great influence with God due to her relational nature. I believe that God has a man for you who will be the man of God, lover and friend you desire, regardless of his past.

Take this as encouragement from me. If God saves a man and delivers him from homosexuality and he wants to love you and live his life out with you, accept him.

PART FOUR

People like you touching people like us:

A message to the church

"A church is not a museum, an exhibition of saints, a showing of pious purebreds. A church is a school, a group of people in various stages of development, from beginners in the Christian life with the dirt of the world still on them to those clad in the white robes of the saints."

-Bishop F. Gerald Ensley,
Methodist Bishop

20

How unbelief, fear and ignorance breed prejudice

ome things never seem to change. In Jesus' day, most folk didn't believe dead people could live again. Mark 5:38-40 records how after a young girl died, Jesus forced everyone (except a few close disciples) out of the resurrection room because they laughed in unbelief. The shocking parallel is that today, many Christians don't believe homosexuals can change.

They believe drug addicts can go clean, they believe prostitutes can get off the streets, they believe drunks can sober up, and they believe convicts can be redeemed from their criminal ways. But why then is it such a stretch of faith to truly believe homosexuals can change? And if they do believe, why not act accordingly by instituting service ministries to help homosexual strugglers live victoriously?

Can homosexuals change? It depends according to what Christian you ask. I won't attempt to define what a

Christian is. Let us just agree that a Christian *should be* a follower of Christ. Knowing that Christianity has become such a pluralistic religion within itself, it is no wonder biblical consensus is almost impossible. If there are 20 Christians asked, most likely there will be 20 different ideologies and theories about the eternal condition of the homosexual. We can easily trace it all to one dubious source: ignorance.

Ignorance is a sin, but seems to be one of the most tolerated sins in the church. Ignorance forces a values-flip. It's like calling the good, evil and the evil, good.

And God help the messengers! There is little appreciation for the bearers of God's standards in contemporary "churchianity". Messengers may have been ordained to expose the lie and educate the church on true Biblical understanding of homosexuality; but quite frequently find themselves either ignored or treated with disdain and in some cases derision. The result? The church continues wandering in a contemporary wilderness, searching for answers but then systematically rejecting them when they come.

Pastor and recording artist Donnie McClurkin said, "We lose many battles due to our IGNORANCE and IGNORING. Most regrettably, not only are we not aware of satan's plans and tactics, but in many cases we seem totally unconcerned."[13]

The church is being led by a generation of people who seem more interested in image and status, than in helping people get free. There is a tremendous amount of hostility in the church today fed by ignorance.

"One of the greatest struggles that any ex-gay will face in the church is the fact that most people will not embrace the idea that he [or she] can change.", said a young black exhomosexual who lives in

Washington DC. The reason, he believes, is because church folk harbor deep seated prejudices against homosexuals.

"I have seen people come forward for deliverance from drugs and alcohol addictions. [Other] people in the congregation just smile to themselves and say 'Thank you Jesus.' During the sermon, when the topic of homosexuality is broached, the same people say 'it's a demon.' The stigma [of coming forward for prayer] would be more than any gay man could take."

More than any other issue the church grapples with, including race and abortion, discussions on homosexuality is clearly the most contentious and confusing. A young black woman who described herself as a Christian said to me she preferred "celibate gay preachers over adulterous heterosexual preachers." Her comment, however strange, represent a growing sentiment in the church especially among young people. It is the jaded voice of cynicism and disillusionment speaking, brought on by unrepentant sexual sins in the ranks. Unfortunately, satan now holds up "celibate homosexuals" as role models of Christian morality.

PARALLELS ON RACE

Though controversial, I see a specific parallel between the struggle over homosexuality in the church and the emerging struggle over institutionalized church-taught racism. Dr. Frederick K.C. Price brilliantly detailed this in his trinity collection of books on racism. He outlined several factors — among many others— that allow racism to fester and receive protected status in the church. This breach of Bible ethic is primarily perpetrated by some white Christians against black Christians. Dr. Price's points include:

1. An insidious doctrine —fashioned out of misinterpreted

Biblical passages~ of racial hatred has been taught and institutionalized in the church.

2. The Christian church has been the leading perpetrator of racism in America.

3. These compounded years of erroneous teaching have so permeated the church and become so rooted that some African Americans have internalized it and accepted it as truth.

4. Although "apologies" have been offered by some parts of the offending parties, there has been no corresponding corrective action.

5. Confronting the perpetrators of the injustice and misrepresentation elicit incredible reactions of ignorance and hostility.

Dr. Price writes, "Maybe the problem with the church is that it has never really found out how God thinks. What people have done is to try to bring God down to their prejudiced level. But we have to bring the level of our ideas up to God's. And if our ideas don't square with God's, we are going to have to change them."[14]

I want to outline those same scenarios Dr. Price used on race and apply them to the current climate regarding homosexuality.

1. An insidious doctrine ~fashioned out of misinterpreted Biblical passages~ of hatred for homosexuals has been taught and institutionalized in the church.

2. The Christian church has been the leading perpetrator of hatred of homosexuals in America.

3. These compounded years of erroneous teaching have so permeated the church and become so rooted that some homosexuals have internalized it and accepted it as truth.

4. There have been no apologies offered by any parts of
    the offending parties, consequently there has been no
    corresponding corrective action.

5. Confronting the perpetrators of the injustice and
    misrepresentation elicit incredible reactions of
    ignorance and hostility.

Doubt cripples the church's attitude towards homosexuals. Just like it killed Isreal's opportunity to get into Canaan, it will surely kill our opportunity to experience true deliverance! Doubt is the devil's adjutant in his plan to keep homosexuals from seeking freedom and likewise the church from pointing them towards it. And we wonder why there are so many gays are clapping, singing and dancing in the church with the no hint of conviction! That tells me one thing.

It's high time for leadership to set the house in order! When disorder is allowed to remain in God's house, all of the devil's children get a bedroom. Spirits of dishonesty, disinterest, disbelief, disruption, discrimination, disobedience, distortion, disturbance, dissension and division run rampant. How can deliverance come forth amid all this? Who can find healing in such a toxic environment?

If we want to get to a healthy place of understanding, it is imperative that we do two things. First, we must identify and confront three poisonous leadership types in the church. I believe these types of leaders are dragging thousands into a hell hole. In their own negative way they have become enablers of that which destroys. They persist in:

1. Promoting homoSINsual relationships.

2. Perpetuating AIDS deaths by cold silence or distorted teachings.

3. Spewing spiRITUAL impotency into the Body of Christ.

If you haven't guessed by now, sin, confusion and rituals water the roots of these leader's arrogant activity.

We know who they are, but we tolerate them and their sacred golden cows.

Secondly, we must get them out of power! Leaders who react with knee-jerk fear, the "tolerance whores" and hardline traditionalists have held the black church under a pathetic sway of mixed-bag spirituality threaten all who desire God to move in the midst of this situation. They threaten us all and they have got to go!

BISHOP FEAR FACTOR, D.D.

When the leader of an "overcomers" ministry for recovering homosexuals at a large Atlanta church had a sexual fall, the whole ministry was summarily shut down. Why? Because the church's leader was faced with an image crisis. It's sad to report, he chose the fear of a tarnished image, rather than to deal righteously with the affected ministry. I can tell you that if a leader in that same church committed adultery, or was arrested for domestic violence, they would not have shut down the entire church.

Just because some miss the mark of holiness, does that mean Christ is powerless to save and keep others who want it? The action of the church's pastor was nothing more than knee-jerk fear. If this standard were applied equally in the church, lots of ministries and auxiliaries would be shut down. Maybe they have never heard that "one monkey don't stop the whole show."

Fear is never a friend to faith. What these leaders fear most is that a ministry to homosexuals will breed hedonistic hookups which will be seen as permissive. Wake up, Rev! Did the Holy Spirit show you in a dream that your church is perfect? People in the church make mistakes and willfully commit sin more often than we'd all like to admit, but the ageless facts of the Bible verify as truth that it does happen. We don't need to look any further than the Corinthian church (1 Cor 6:9-11) to realize that there are all types of EXsinners inside. It was all happening there! But it seems like with "exgay" ministries, an uncontrollable fear sets in. Preachers portray or view ministry to the sexually broken as a sacred privilege, much like a piece of candy given to a good little boy, only to be swiftly snatched from him if he misbehaves.

At the first sign of sexual impropriety, they envision a den of hedonism where everyone coming to the ministry will end up naked and perverted on the floor. Their one-size-fit-all solution? SHUT IT DOWN! The truth is, hedonistic hookups are not the norm, but rather the exception. Shutting down a complete ministry is a sad case of the end attempting to justify the means. The fear factor actually slams shut the door of healing in someone else's face. It locks down the authority of the pastor to assess a situation and then remove the perpetrators, rather than engage in mass punishment.

They would do well to follow the level headed advice of Paul to the Corinthian church leaders: you deal with this individual or else when I come I'm going to deal with him (1 Corinthians 5:1-5). He never issued any orders to shut the church down. Those striving to overcome their homosexuality should not be treated as invisible stepchildren.

Wherever there exists such fear in our dealings with homosexuality in the church, it makes it easy for others to ridicule and attack homosexuals. This is unGodly. Since I have been in the black church all my life, I can only speak about what I have seen. Yes, of course it happens in white churches, but we have an epidemic on our hands! That's why in the confusion and fear fed ignorance it's so easy for some African American preachers to make cruel jokes and casually toss gutter remarks at homosexuals.

If the preacher gets started on homosexuals, the church is transformed into Sunday morning at Def Jam Comedy. Some sinners become the brunt of the preacher's Sunday morning joke-a-thon. After all, the Bible says they are reprobates, right? And a reprobate can't possibly change, right? This warped interpretation is what has plagued and hindered our churches from real outreach to homosexuals. This creates a view of gays as "abstract sinners." Misinterpretations of the Bible portray homosexuals as freaks, without a heart and soul. Dr. Price pointed out the same tactics used against blacks.

Quoting from white writer Charles Carroll (who pontificates that "the Negro is one of the ape family") Price writes:

"This is why things are the way they are today in America between black and white people. Carroll believed that my family and I and all of our black friends and neighbors ~indeed every black person on the planet~ are animals, that we are the Bible's "beast[s] of the field." He told his wife and children, and his children told their children, his readers told their wives or husbands and children, and their children told their children."[15]

This is also exactly why a great majority church today DOES NOT believe homosexuals can truly change! Lies have gone on for decades and generations unchallenged. They have been slow cooked with old wives fables and misinterpreted scripture. So when an "intelligent" and "popular" black pastor says "homosexuals can be saved, but not converted", what else can people think except that "Bobby" is doomed to a life of abomination?

Why do some African American church leaders bristle when they are told homosexuality is a problem in the church? Why don't they get angry over the tongue-talking liars and the dancing tithe thieves in the pews? I believe its because of the fear factor. Fear that they may lose control. And fear that the "controversy" of homosexuality will damage their neat little packages of smiling families and manicured religion.

THE TOLERANCE WHORES

Adding to the confusion are the "tolerance whores" who masquerade as preachers. These weak-watered talking heads are willing to let anything and everything slither in and say it is a child of God. Operating under the guise of fighting "homophobia", or eradicating "social injustice", some ministers have remodeled their churches into havens of perversion, denying the very grace that brought them.[17]

The tolerance whores are easily recognizable. They use terms such as "diversity" and "inclusion", words with ulterior meanings created by wolves to gain access to the flock of God. The tolerance whores lay on the guilt trip thick. They cite examples of unjust slavery, the denial of women in ministry and unlawful interracial marriages to support their bogus claims of including obstinate, unrepentant and troublesome (OUT) gays and lesbians.

It's a sad commentary that some preachers have allowed God's house of prayer to become a den of thieves. Its sad, but true that many so-called houses of worship are nothing more than hideouts for thieves and spiritual chameleons. A den that has become a home of comfort in sin, instead of a place of challenge against sin.

You can identify tolerance whores because they will quickly put the "OUT" gays and lesbians into positions of influence and authority. They are laden with guilt over perceived injustices, so compensation ends up as overcompensation. Armed with this power, these gays will stifle and kill anything from God that calls them from their sin.

At a popular black Baptist church in Waco, a woman whose son had been delivered from homosexuality began sharing around the church of her son's wonderful conversion. That was a mistake! The church, however was home to a faction of educated gays. As soon as the word of the poor sister's testimony reached their ears, they rushed to the church's pastor and demanded that he silence this woman. The pastor, a newly ordained tolerance whore, responded by removing the sister from all her offices and eventually drummed her out of the church. Gays in the church complained that she was "in their business."

Rev. Kenneth Samuel, pastor of Victory Baptist Church (now Victory Church) in the Atlanta suburb of Stone Mountain is a recent tolerance whore. According to news release, Samuel "convinced himself" that "homophobia" should be fought as hard as racism as the basis for his newfound acceptance of open homosexuals into his church.

Samuel represents the core type of tolerance whores, who use every indefensible excuse possible to flood the church with openly gay members. "Open" signifies that the individual has no problem with others knowing they are gay. They further believe being open about their sexual dysfunction is a badge of integrity.

Samuel told the Associated Press, "we are not being untrue to our faith by affirming all people."[16] What is meant by "affirming" and "all people"? Well, in the tolerance whore's mentality, the terms are simply metaphors for acceptance of homosexuality.

The pastor quickly went to work justifying homosexual sin acceptance as a "outgrowth" of racism. This ideology is part and parcel of the new doctrine of gay and gay friendly theologians who contend that the acceptance of homosexual sin is a social justice cause. It may well be, but the Gospel's bottom line has always been the salvation of the soul, not the eradication of societal injustice. We could right all the wrongs of societal injustice, but where would that leave us if we are not in relationship with God?

Tolerance whores spend all of their time at HIV/AIDS seminars, ecumenical meetings and gay rights conferences instead of in the Word of God. "Her" goal is to gain a reputation as a "progressive church" but in doing so the tolerance whore ends up spreading her legs for every filthy sin that gives her a nickel. Soon, infected by the discharge of all her whorish associations, she lashes out, attacking the very nature (purity, holiness) of Christ.

You'll know tolerance whores by the "enlightened" words they speak. Key phrases in the spiritual vocabulary of the tolerance whore:

"liberation theology"
"radical ministry of Jesus"
"inclusive gospel"
"tolerance and diversity"
"all God's children"
"open and affirming."

These socially constructed and acceptable wordplays, although harmless when evoked in the right spirit, have nonetheless become weapons in the arsenal of individuals intent on altering the standards of God's word. We have to be ever so cautious of what we rush to embrace and offer to others. Like the fruit Eve ate in the garden, it could spell serious trouble for those who do not understand the severity of their implications for the church.

Doctrines espoused by these types of leaders are rife with error.

The Bible identifies them as "doctrines of devils." Such doctrines are marked for their emphasis and promotion of sexuality and sensuality (Jude 18,19).

These beguiling doctrines of inclusion and tolerance are misguided as well as problematic. In order to make sinners comfortable they mute scripture that call for self control and rejection of worldly lust. To them grace is synonymous with self pleasure.

AIN'T NO HOMOSEXUALS IN MY CHURCH!

I worked for almost 10 years in the airline industry. Needless to say that type of job brings you into contact with many people of various persuasions. I've dealt with everyone from exCNNer Catherine Crier to Kurt Carr to Julian Bond to Dr. Tony Evans. I made an attempt to listen to everyone who has something to say as I handled their travel transactions. Some ministers are adamant that they don't have to deal with homosexuals because there simply are none in their congregations. Is that the truth? Not according to one preacher who shared with me on my job one day.

Our conversation started out on a sane note, even though I was trying to hold to my 3 minute rule of taking care of customers. The 50ish looking gentlemen, dressed in a dark suit, told me that he was a preacher. He added that he *used to be* COGIC. Now, he really had my interest. I asked why he was no longer with the COGIC.

He leaned towards me and looked around as if he were about to reveal top military secrets. "Too many sissies!", he hissed. "They're everywhere! In the choirs, pulpits, everywhere!" I could tell by the look on his face that he was dead serious. After his revelation, he took a step back from my counter and looked at me, apparently shocked at his own words. His temples pumped in and out. *Someone has really pushed his buttons*, I thought.

Are there "too many sissies" in the church? According to this last enemy of knowledge, they don't exist. Church leaders who follow a hardline traditionalist approach are so blind, they deny homosexuality exists altogether. Imagine a pastor saying "we're not gonna have no sissies up in our choir! No! not in this church!" But seated behind him are some of the most obviously effeminate men you'd ever want to see. Don't believe it? I wouldn't have either, unless I had witnessed it.

I saw with my own eyes the son of a leading preacher show up in church dressed as a woman. His father apparently didn't recognize him. What happens when the church is subjected to these blind leaders?

First, they create an atmosphere ripe for hypocrisy. By stating that there "ain't no homosexuals" in their church, that leader is lying to his or her congregation about the reality of sin. Churches have all kinds of sinners in them, and there is certainly no shortage of homosexual sinners in the pew. Sin is a reality and homosexuality is a snapshot of that reality. The church shouldn't deny it, but get aware and then prepare to meet it with ministry. I tend to think that many leaders desperately *want* to believe there are no "sissies" in their church, but that's simply not the case.

Secondly, hardliners see the admission of homosexuality in the church as a confession of failure and weakness. They would rather be cast into the den of hungry lions rather than admit some members of their congregations have same-gender sexual issues.

WE MUST CHANGE!

We must change! The truth is if homosexuals, lesbians, transvestites, bisexuals, pederasts, transsexuals and all in that spectrum of the sexually deficient are to find lasting wholeness, it must come through the fellowship of believers. There is no other way! God has ordained for the church to be the river of healing waters for the sin sick and the soul wounded.

Pastor Terry Weir, formerly of New York's Brooklyn Tabernacle said to us in our very first *Hope for Healing in the Truth* conference, "God can deliver every homosexual who wanted to be delivered, right now. The question is when He does, what church will disciple them, love them and lead them into being a part of the body of Christ?"

That's the question that should echo in the ear of every pastor who says he or she wants to know the heart of God: What are you going to do with them, once God brings them to you?

Like me, you have probably heard all your life that the church is supposed to be a "hospital for the sick." True, but too many patients are being told to heal themselves or just get a spiritual makeovers.

Many churches these days are not hospitals, just make-over factories! Let's just tell the truth and shame the devil, shall we?!! I'm sure you've seen those Jenny Jones makeover shows. "Susie" has bad self-esteem and dresses way too sexy, but with a little rebuke, a new dress and some makeup, she's a brand new woman, right? The church's adoption of this sick mentality is nothing more than religious psychobabble when it comes to homosexuality.

The average black church has NO DESIRE to reach out to homosexuals! Sure, they know they're there, but operate based on the hands-off approach. I heard one well-known Bishop, doing a guest spot on BET's now canceled *Tavis Smiley* show say (that in his church) "we treat homosexuality like every other sin."

Sorry, Bishop, that's a clear equivocation of the facts, not to mention a weak defense. How, in God's name, can a church tout their special outreaches for the sins of drug addicts, prostitutes, gang members, unwed mothers and alcoholics, but refuse ministry to gays? I applaud the church for taking care of folks caught in predicaments of homelessness, hunger and computer illiteracy. Why, there's even a black church in Los Angeles which maintains a breast cancer ministry! Great! But excuse me please, when did homosexuals ask to be left off the list?

Few churches will make any real attempts to reach out to men and women —*even in their congregations*— who struggle against homosexual thoughts, feelings, or relationships. This happens because unbelief, fear and ignorance breed prejudice.

If the church *didn't* believe they could change the prostitute's sexual proclivities, they wouldn't try to help her. If they *didn't* believe they could make a difference in the life of the young man selling dope on the streets, they wouldn't go after him. If they *didn't* believe a young woman who'd had a baby out of wedlock could somehow ever become a productive member of the church community, they wouldn't reach out to her. On the other hand, if they truly *believed* God could change the homosexual, then an outreach to homosexuals would be on the "A" list, instead of no list at all.

RECOGNIZING THE SERIOUS TROUBLE FACING YOUNG PEOPLE

Do you want to know who suffers most behind this intoxicating blend of hypocrisy? If you guessed young people, you guessed right.

Youth have inherited the ignorance of the church's cookie box teachings on sexuality. It's no wonder abortion, homosexuality, premarital sex and other sexual based sins have found a home among the youth of the church. Young folks are also under siege from the world's images and messages. Like a broken record, society says to young people "You must feel good at any and all costs."

The world, with its shattered moral compass, preaches to young people that sexual conduct is relative. The world's message to them is that no one (God included) has a right to judge anyone else's private actions. A sinister new definition of tolerance has gripped everything from the classroom to the corporate boardroom: "I don't care if I'm destroying my life, just support me and accept me in it." Out of that destructive mantra, spews forth school killings, homosexual involvement at earlier ages, young mothers who can birth a child one minute and toss it into a garbage can the next and so on.

The confusion and ensuing suffering comes ~not from homophobia or intolerance~ but from young people believing that they are the master of their own fate and destiny. Embracing this falsehood intensifies internal struggles for young people struggling against same-sex desires. And the church does little, if anything, to counteract this powerful drug being injected directly into their veins.

There is a critical need for solid, candid and truthful teaching on sex and sexuality. Even more importantly than teaching them to be race conscious or how to get the dollar, young people need to know how to possess their bodies in sanctification and honor. They need to be aware that neither the condom lie nor the safe sex message has worked and will never work because there is no such thing as SAFE SIN with God. Wake up, sin is never safe!

I can't begin to tell you how many young people in church I have encountered who have displayed this incredibly deceptive line of thought. Unless they said so, you'd never know they were in any way connected to the church. When churches begin to teach a holistic sexual doctrine, young people will be empowered to make choices that not only will save their physical lives, but preserve their souls. The current lack of teaching severely hinders youth seeking Godly answers to sexuality issues from their church leaders.

Not only must leaders endeavor to talk about heterosexual issues, but teach on issues of gender confusion, homosexual dysfunction, and overcoming sexual fantasies. If we draw back, and a look at today's youth suggest that we have, then secular organizations like Planned Parenthood and other so-called "sexperts" will teach our children destructive sexual behavior. Because this generation of youth stand to be the most prophetic and powerful yet, they are also the most targeted for destruction. I believe out of the babies and teenagers we see, will come some of God's greatest generals. We already know that satan will attempt to destroy them at an early age like he did those of Moses' and Jesus' time.

Respected Christian author and counselor Josh McDowell, says in his book, *Youth in Crisis*, "Unfortunately the church is often the last place struggling young people turn to at such times. They hide their fears or feelings, afraid of being condemned or labeled abnormal. They imagine no pastor, youth pastor, or other Christian could possibly understand what they're going through, so they suffer in silence, sometimes with tragic results."

In 1998, Christian author Don Schmierer of California wrote a ground breaking book entitled "An Ounce of Prevention: Preventing the homosexual condition in today's youth." The book quickly advanced the belief that homosexuality in youth was a preventable thing, IF parents, educators and religious leaders took time to invest in young people. Schmierer passionately laid out his case that healthy family and peer relationships, early recognition of warning signs— particularly same-sex feelings of inferiority and isolation— would turn the tide being nurtured by the gay rights movement.

After many years of observing youth behavior in and out of the homosexual lifestyle, some in church, some not, I discovered there were at least seven (maybe more) warning signs of homosexual conditioning in young people. One of them — an infusion of unfamiliar words and phrases into their vocabulary— we have already talked about.

I am a parent, too. Although I don't want to be a "snoop" into my children's lives, nor do I want to dictate the course they should choose, I have a God-given obligation to watch for their souls. Getting an education is good and important. Choosing the right career path is great, but learning to possess their bodies in sanctification and honor (1 Thessalonians 4:1-5) is God's will.

But what exactly do you need to observe? What warning signs can help a parent recognize a homosexual condition in their child?

▶ First, if a young person is involved or bonding with someone of the same sex in an unhealthy way, there is a strong tendency to engage in denial. He or she *refuses to see the "friend's" faults realistically.* All humans innately and ideally should have healthy interdependence on others. It's God-given. Yes, we all have to depend on each other for something. However, when people in relationships have ruinous secrets, which homosexual relationships tend to portray, your child's refusal to see obvious faults in the other person is a tale-tell sign that something is wrong.

▶ *Exhibits an intimacy with the friend that causes others to feel uncomfortable.* This suggests that sexual conduct may have already occurred. It further suggests that the relationship has begun developing an emotional bond, something that can't easily be broken. The couple's lack of public discretion in the presence of others could mean what's been done in private, is now strong enough to be public, even if others are uncomfortable with witnessing the behavior.

▶ *Becomes unusually defensive when asked about the relationship.* Couples, who are in the process of bonding, sometimes become defensive when questioned about the merits of their relationship. Homosexuality almost always creates a false sense of love and acceptance. If there have been secret yearnings for same-sex exploration, this relationship probably meets the need for that type of attention. Many times it's translated into an "us vs them" mentality. Watch for frequent signs of jealousy, possessiveness, and exclusivism.

▶ *Writes secret poetry or music about the friend.* Should any 13 or 14 year-old be *that* passionate about someone outside the family unit? This is a strong sign that the other person may be older. An older person's influence and false promises of love and concern trap youth into equally false desires to return these feelings. I believe the element of secrecy signals dangerously wrong motives.

▶ *Emotional teeter-tottering.* Your child's first brush with homosexual intimacy will spawn a flurry of deep emotional conflicts. While the teen may experience strong feelings of guilt, awakened desires and curiosity also trouble them. The two discordants (desire and guilt) war against each other, creating an atmosphere ripe for suicidal thoughts to take shape.

▶ *Drastic changes in clothing styles that reflect aspects of gay lifestyle.* Males tend to display signs much earlier than females, however with an increasingly higher profile of masculine women, young girls are beginning to see "role models" they too can emulate. The "gay lifestyle" is a subculture that has devised its own dress code. While it's true most gays dress no differently than heterosexuals, there are still several "styles" which point to homosexuality. For a young person being seduced into this arena, dressing for acceptance is a powerful factor! Take notice of drastic hair color changes and the *way* clothes are worn, especially if they "show off" certain body parts such as the groin or buttocks. If a young woman tapes or hides the natural contours of her breasts, she may be uncomfortable with looking feminine.

God's people must get back to the business of believing Him. Why have we even allowed salvation of the homosexual to become an "impossible" situation? Can it be that our unbelief has kept us wandering in this wilderness of ignorance lo these many years?

The other disheartening aspect of unbelief is that some leaders in the black church perpetuate it by playing court to extremes. Black parishioners are continually fed a Spirit-starved diet of carnal theology on homosexuality. Most of it could be referred to simply as "pulpit jockism". This phenomenon of carnal intelligence is the product of years of silence. What did Bishop Charles Harrison Mason and other early pentecostal pioneers teach on homosexuality?

One of their founding pentecostal contemporaries, Charles Fox Parham had that problem. He was reportedly arrested in 1907 for "homosexual acts" which became public and eventually caused Parham to lose lifelong ministerial credibility behind it[18].

Too many of God's ministers are still peeling off *bon mots*, clever little sayings such as "God didn't create Adam and Steve, He created Adam and Eve"! With over 25 explicit and implicit Biblical references[19] addressing the homosexual condition, it is inexcusable and unacceptable for leaders to utter such divisive and immature statements.

I've personally heard some of the leading evangelists, bishops and pastors, astute men in their own right, speak out on everything from affirmative action to the Clinton debacle. Yet, none of them can bring themselves to address homosexuality in a holistic way. Many of those ministers who speak about homosexuality, do so in dereliction to their calling to feed the sheep with knowledge (Jeremiah 3:15). Judge for yourself. Can you find any redemptive value in the following remarks?

▶ *"That's sick wanting to be a homosexual.", said a Houston-based evangelist. "I feel sorry for the brother who's never known the love of a woman."*[18]

▶ *In Georgia, a popular radio preacher bragged on air, "If any faggots come to my church, me and the brothers are gonna hog-tie em and pray those demons out of them!"*[20]

▶ *" A homosexual cannot be converted," snapped an angry COGIC evangelist at a New Year's Eve revival meeting in Berkley, California.*

*"He can be saved, but not converted." Amid the hoots and howls of the
church audience, he repeatedly referred to lesbians as "nasty
scoundrels"[22]*

This is not to say that these men are bad people or they don't have
a relationship with God. These are just sad examples of spiritual
ignorance. I marvel that men of their stature could have nothing more
to say than this sort of mean-spirited mush. And by the way, none of
the above statements have any scriptural foundation.

I will say to them: stop hiding behind your flowing ecclesiastical
robes and your profound pronouncements of rhema revelations. It's
an exciting menu, but who can grow healthy on cake and ice cream
everyday? Stop rejecting those who need you the most. Most of all,
stop the cycle of prejudice you strengthen by your fear and
misinformation to the flock of God. God will hold you accountable
for the souls that you drive away from Him. He has made it crystal
clear that their blood will be required at your hands.

21
Touching
a Dead Man

*P*erhaps it was shaping up to be one of those
typical Sundays. Perhaps it was just time for
God to show me some things. At any rate,
during our Sunday School lesson, an innocent little
question abruptly got me to wondering.

One brother wanted to know why Jesus didn't help
Lazarus to get free. The Holy Spirit really startled my
mind. You have to understand, I'm the type of person
whose mind continually churns with thoughts, questions
and ideas. Everything that's said to me I take and
analyze, either for storage or disposal. Either I can use or
I'll lose it. This was something I definitely could use! I'm
still trying to figure out if that's a curse or a blessing!

Later in the day after I was home, I hurriedly turned
to the passage in John 11:31-44. It was a familiar passage
of scripture I'd read many times before, but this time the
Spirit of God quickened a revelation from it. I believe
some revelations, God hides from us, because it's just
not time to be opened. It's very possible that having read

184

the Bible many times, the revelation was there all the time, but to me, it was obscured, waiting patiently until God's time was ripe. Then, by opening it up to me, through the Spirit's quickening, it could have maximum impact, not only on my life, but stretch way beyond me to touch others.

As I read, I was immediately mesmerized by the implications of the story of Jesus, the dead man Lazarus and the people. Then, I was stunned at the spiritual wealth of this simple passage of a dead man who lived again. It was truly one of those moments of absolute awe at the power of God's Word.

I knew that in order to understand the question set forth, I had to first replay it in the context of my struggles. By this time in my life, I had experienced a steady growth and maturity in my walk with the Lord. But I needed to capitulate for a moment. I needed to ask myself the same questions others who struggle to overcome the vertigo of homosexual feelings ask themselves. Why is it so hard for the church to understand what I'm going through? Why do they back away from helping me overcome my problems? Why won't these feelings just go away and never return? Will I ever truly be free and what will it take to get there?

In my reflective state, it seemed like we all have been consigned to some sort of "pentecostal purgatory". In this contrived place, the rules are a matter of expediency. If you just shout and dance hard enough, the church will accept you as a free man or woman. If you fluently ply the air with unknown tongues, you will be a deeply spiritual person in the eyes of the church. If you are always in attendance to every service, then everyone will know you are dedicated to the Lord. If you do all these things, you can be totally free of all your homosexual desires forever. In other words, you too, can live happily ever after. But is it really that simple?

Does the Bible really promise this kind of spiritual utopia for any believer? If those are the qualifications, then I have shouted. I have danced. I have spoken in tongues and been to church every time I could. But this is a struggle and it ain't easy. I still struggle to keep my thoughts pure. Don't we all do that? I still can't explain why I have to try to measure myself by other men in the church. An enormous amount of fear and mistrust is directed at my ex-lesbian sisters from other church women. I guess all we are saying is "brother, sister can we depend on you to help us out?"

In the church today, that could be a loaded question. I now realize, after I took off my rose colored sanctified spectacles, that a great deal of the church body struggles with one thing or another. Some people have devised a way to conceal their struggles, thereby giving the appearance that everything is OK in their lives. I won't begrudge them that, but it does smudge the reality of living for Christ. The reality is that no one has attained such an exalted state of holiness, that they are above failure, sin (omission and commission) and faults. I'll say it again, NO ONE. We all have some dead areas in our lives that need the touch of Christ.

This ex-dead man Lazarus faced a similar problem homosexuals (from society in general) and exhomosexuals have in the church today. He faced the same type of unbelieving, cynical religion mongers. Yes, he heard the gossip, but he came on out of the tomb anyway! Yes, he saw through the cracks in his head bandages, the incredulous stares of the people, but he kept on stumbling out!

That's exactly what we have to do. Keep moving. Once Christ calls your name, you will never be the same again. Once the door to that tomb of homosexuality opens, there should be no turning back. Yes, there will be unfriendly faces, and unkind whispers and hateful actions, but the people had no power to call you. Christ called your name and brought you forth. And even in your hobbled state, you should press your way to Him, find Him and fall to His feet in gratitude! Had it been up to them, they would have left you in the grave to finish decaying! But you, like Lazarus are alive! Now, what do you do with your freedom?

Lazarus was completely wrapped from head to toe in the garments of the past. But he was alive. Regardless of what he appeared to be, there was life in him, and that life was given to him by Jesus, *for the glory of God.* Some of you may still have that lisp in your voice, but you have the life of Christ in you.

Some of you may still struggle to stand and walk the way you were born to do, but there is life in you. Some of you may not understand how you will make it, but what is important is that you know you are alive. Yes, there may even be a "smell" of the past lingering around you, causing others to congratulate themselves. They believed their "spirit" told them something wasn't right about you. That's all right, I'm here to deliver the GOOD NEWS to you man and to you woman, YOU ARE FREE from that tomb!

How many times have we judged people by what we saw instead of what God had done in their hearts? I know that it grieves the Holy Spirit, because we never give them a chance. It happened to me before.

I was at church when someone told me that I had a phone call. When I answered it, a young woman's voice patiently explained to me that she had read the 1998 *Charisma* article "Let's stop hiding from the pain: homosexuality and the black church." Our ministry WITNESS! was featured in it.

I listened, of course very humbled that this young woman was inspired by our story. She told me she was calling from Atlanta and her name was Michael. I thanked her and offered prayer to bless her. I began praying "Lord bless this young woman and keep her in your care, strengthen..." Midways the sentence, Michael interrupted me and protested, "I'm not a woman, I'm a man!"

Needless to say, I was absolutely mystified. I distinctly heard a woman's voice on the other end of the line, but this person now said *he* was a man. I quickly apologized and continued praying for him. Michael?, I thought puzzled. Afterwards I set up an appointment to speak with him again on the phone.

Since coming to know Michael in 1998, he has been a tremendous inspiration to me. He braved serious odds to leave his former lifestyle of cross dressing to come to Christ and today he is continuing life as a strong Christian man. I remember telling him, never to feel less than other men because his voice was soft. I felt that God had let it remain to challenge the very perceptions of judgment the church routinely engages in. Michael's testimony is wonderful and is proof that God is still calling dead men out of the tombs.

Did Lazarus really need help? Yes, he certainly did. Jesus' command to "loose him and let him go" was not designed to produce an immediate spiritual response, but was crafted to produce a natural response of man helping man. We all need help in our Christian walk, especially those who are wobbling out of years of sinful lifestyle habits.

No one criticizes a baby taking those first few precious steps when he or she falls. Actually, it's a time when everyone in the room rejoices, because of the POTENTIAL the baby is demonstrating. When my youngest son Charles *finally* begin to walk, Dee and I were almost as happy as we were the day he was born (Charles is another book, so I won't go into that!) If the baby falls (which he will) you encourage him to get up and try again. What if we did homosexuals coming out of their lifestyle like that? What if we encouraged them, even when they fell, not fearing that we were "giving them a license to sin"? Oh, what a change we would see!

But it seems our brothers and sisters are not willing to afford us that luxury. We are unfairly held to double standards of judgment. I was in Seattle, back in 1998 for the Exodus International North American conference and talked to a young woman whom I had grown up with. I was so glad to see her again after all those years. She and her brother now lived in Seattle and it was a great reunion. She had several male friends in the church whom she believed had been gay. But some things about them troubled her.

"Darryl, why don't they just stop twisting and talking like that if they are really delivered?", she asked. She really couldn't understand why they could not just drop it all and be perfect "men". I believe her question was innocent and sincere. I imagine someone questioned whether Lazarus was really alive, too. *Why is he still wearing those stinky grave clothes? Why does he walk like that? Is he really alive?* If the way a person looks or acts causes us to feel uncomfortable, does that mean they are not truly changed? According to 1 Samuel 16:7, the truth of the change is within the heart, which God considers.

> *But the Lord said to Samuel, do not consider his appearance or his height, for I have rejected him. The Lord does not look at the things man looks at. Man looks at the outward appearance, but the Lord look at the heart.*

WHY JESUS DIDN'T HELP LAZARUS

It's amazing to me, in the passage dealing with Lazarus, that we are allowed to see Jesus be moved with such visceral emotion. The Jews themselves could also see how visibly shaken Jesus was over his friend's death. "See how he loved him", they said as Jesus wept. I have had a close friend die (see chapter 5 on my friend Michael's suicide).

And you no doubt have lost someone very close to you. It's a pain whose depth that can only be understood if you have suffered it. We all long to keep close those we love, but somehow we know that someday they will be taken away from us. Perhaps Jesus' humanity felt this encroaching loss, but like in the Garden of Gethsemane he fell back on his spiritual understanding and remembered Lazarus' death was for the glory of God. It was the will of God.

This may help us to understand then John 11:35, the Bible's shortest, yet most poignant verse. Jesus wept. But even with the obvious pain Jesus felt, it didn't prompt him to lift one finger and assist Lazarus. Lazarus, one of his most intimate friends is stumbling out of a tomb after four days, but Jesus does not run to him nor make any known overtures to embrace his friend. Is this any way for a so-called friend to act? Shouldn't Jesus have went running towards his friend, throwing his arms about his neck, kissing him and weeping for joy? I'm sure he wanted to.

But His eyes are on us. He had done all he was going to do. He demonstrated his power to call life out of death. That was the act of God. By calling the name of a dead man, Jesus defied every natural and spiritual law known. He synchronized and harnessed the breath of God and blew it into Lazarus' lifeless body. He rebuked the encroachment of decay. He commanded the angel of death to cease in his tracks. Truly, power belongs to God!

Now, Jesus was about to issue another astonishing decree, this time to the "church" standing by.

"Loose him and let him go!", commanded Jesus.

This command was of a different nature than the first. The first, *Lazarus, come forth!* was a spiritual occurrence. The second however, was a practical command, but no less powerful.

There was a hesitation stirring in the minds of the people. With the exception of his stumbling, Lazarus looked as if he were a dead man. It was, at once, a hard and wonderful sight. They were suspended between tradition and fearful superstition and what they had witnessed Jesus do many times before. Could he count on them to obey him now? They clearly heard him say "loose him", but obedience to that command complicated matters.

The people knew the strict levitical law stipulated that anyone who touched or came near a dead body was defiled and rendered ceremoniously unclean (Lev 22:3-5). This law was of extreme importance especially to the priesthood, because they were charged with being intercessors for the people.

The fear caused them to forget Jesus said he had not come to destroy the law, but to fulfill it (Matthew 5:17). The law, Jesus taught was fulfilled in love. I believe that it was. Jesus removed the Old Testament imposed physical sentence of death for sins, while maintaining the standard of acceptable moral living. His command was a call and a challenge to change. He called them and He is calling us into a change to love by actions.

So, then what stood staring at Jesus was a church who believed *in him*, but found it difficult to obey him. This left Lazarus for a while stymied and suspended in a quandary of his own: how was he to be completely free without the assistance of those "who stood by"? How are these delivered homosexuals going to be completely free without the assistance of the church?

If you notice, Jesus didn't say "pray for him" or "fast for him." He didn't say give him an offering. He didn't say bake him a German chocolate cake or invite him to a church prayer meeting. What he said, very clearly was "loose him and let him go." The act of loosing Lazarus required close, personal, and physical involvement. His command appealed to the compassion in the people. How could they stand and watch someone struggle with the intentions of getting free and not reach out to help them? Yes, the person(s) helping Lazarus would most likely smell some of the stench of death he had just walked out of. But such is the stench of sin and the sinful life.

Deep felt compassion for anyone in the throes of a struggle for their very life, their very existence is the hallmark of the ministry of the Chief Shepherd. And compassion should be one of the primary controlling emotions of all pastoral ministry. Yes, I said emotion. Paul wrote in Hebrews 4:15 that this same Jesus is "touched by the feelings of our infirmities." He sympathizes with our weaknesses. He understands how and why we feel the way we do when pressed by temptations.

The story of Lazarus is a blatant attempt to teach his heart of compassion. He wanted us to understand that our level of effectiveness in helping the sexually broken is directly connected to the physical proximity of our ministry.

Understandably then, the church can never expect to be effective in exhorting exhomosexuals when ministry is conducted with a "10 foot pole" mentality. Demonstrative mercy and compassion must be positioned close by those who stand to benefit most from it. Over and over we see Jesus in the gospels touching, healing and being moved emotionally as the model of what works with people who are damaged, bruised, broken and bound. In fact, this is what God anointed Jesus to do (Acts 10:38).

If you have ever asked can a person be delivered and yet be bound, here you have your answer. Lazarus was delivered from death, but is yet bound hand and foot in the clothes of death. The definition of deliverance is to "rescue from danger". Deliverance rescues you from imminent danger. But getting outside the door of the tomb is never the end of it all, rather it is just the beginning. There is a lot that must be done once you come out of the cave of sin and its decaying consequences.

However, it was to the people standing by to whom he directed his command. In other words, stop standing by and get involved in loosing someone. There's no special invitation needed, just leave all of your superstitions and traditions behind and help someone get out of the clothes of the past lifestyle.

Praying for someone is fine and honorable. Church folks are quick to say "prayer changes things". You must understand, however that prayer cannot change things, circumstances or people. That's never been the purpose of prayer to act as a arbitrator of our human desires. Prayer in it's purest form sets you in agreement with the will of the Father God, and HE changes things, circumstances and people. If this were not the case, we could manipulate things, circumstances and people according to our feelings, which James 4:3 declares is praying "amiss". Admittedly, we are not always in harmony with God's will.

That's why God is calling on you to get involved in helping homosexuals to be free.

I will never accuse the church, I love it too much, but love requires that we acknowledge and dutifully work on our weak areas and strengthen them against the enemy, who does accuse us. The church owes a debt of repentance to the many homosexual men and women it has lied on, laughed at, talked about, rejected and mistreated. The church owes God a repentance, too. To a great extent, His command has not been obeyed. He told His church to loose them. Instead, we have laid the blame on homosexuals, trying to satisfy and justify the guilt of our own disobedience.

Like old man John on the Isle of Patmos, I too, for a brief moment was caught up in the Spirit to behold a wondrous sight. I heard Jesus calling the names of homosexuals and countless numbers came stumbling out of the tombs of their sins and into new life. Thousands of them, like myself, haltingly moved out into the sunshine of His love, squinting our eyes and searching deeply for a friendly face which would say, "Can I help you brother? Are you going to make it, sister? Let me help to loose you."

Yes, we heard the Savior's powerful voice call out our names, but where are those who stood by? Like those people in that day, many in the church today stand by scrutinizing our every move.

We must understand that Jesus has done his job. Prayer is in order, but don't pray as substitution to your responsibility to me or others like me Don't use prayer as a way to get around obedience to God. Please pray for us, but back your prayer up with action. John 11:44 can only be revealed in obedience.

I believe with fervent faith that when the church He left to exercise the ministry of reconciliation recognizes this need, we'll see fewer homosexuals hiding in pulpits and choirs. We'll witness many more testimonies of healing and deliverance from homosexuality. We'll see more ministers preaching healing messages instead of wounding messages.

Lazarus was dead only four days; I lay dead for 11 years. Yet, the power of Christ and His passionate love for the both of us raised us and brought us out. It's good to know that after all these years, there are some people who are not afraid to get involved.

What about you? Are you ready to touch me? Just as a baby craves and needs the touch of its mother to develop healthy bonding, I need your touch. There's no need to be afraid of me, I'm your brother who was once dead, but now I am alive. When you fail to touch, refuse to get involved, and reject us your brothers and sisters, you fail at life's most basic purpose. And that is to create, sustain and enjoy relationship.

APPENDIX
Reality Kills:
The Profiles

I don't think that anyone who grasps the
Biblical explanation of sin, can or will argue
against it's destructive and deadly results.
Some have said that AIDS doesn't discriminate, but
that's only partially true. Sin, however has affected the
entire human race - past, present and future. It matters
not how famous a person may be, or how gifted and
talented they are, unchecked sin will devour their lives
like a raging fire until everything is consumed. Even
then, the residual effects of sin which bear so heavily
upon the whole world will continue until the Lord
Jesus returns. We know this because the Apostle Paul
wrote in Romans 8:22,23 (NIV):

> We know the whole creation has been groaning as
> in the pains of childbirth right up until the present
> time. Not only so but we ourselves, who have been
> the firstfruits of the Spirit, groan inwardly as we
> wait eagerly for our adoption as sons, the
> redemption of our bodies.

There is a deep longing to be set free from every

vestige of sin.

TO JUDGE OR NOT TO JUDGE,
THAT'S THE QUESTION

When speaking of the sin in the lives of others, Christ cautioned us first, not to be judgmental or to hold ourselves up as more righteous than we think we are. While I'm here may I say a word about being judgmental? It has become such a lightning rod against Christians, that many are literally afraid to stand up for God and His righteous standards. I want to attack that fear that comes from the enemy. It's apparent to me that satan has perverted the words of Jesus and caused much confusion.

Many of you have heard someone remark ~with acrimonious self righteousness~ on more than one occasion, "How dare you judge me!?" This imperious question seems to be the command to cease all questions and silence all concerns instantly. But is it so? Is this the proverbial "brick wall" for saints? If not, then what are the boundaries for judging our fellow man? Have you ever wondered why there is a book called "Judges" in the Bible. Do you remember that ominous verse which ends the book? I'll refresh your memory. "In those days there was no king (administrator of the law) in Isreal: every man did that which was right in his own eyes (verse 25).

One cannot help but wonder what Paul meant by his rebuke in 1 Corinthians 6:2 when he says, "Do you not know that the saints will judge the world? And if the world will be judged by you, are you unworthy to judge even the smallest matters?" The purpose of this rebuke was to get the church to handle matters based on evidence and arguments and dispense godly justice. In other words, they were to make a distinct call between what is right and wrong.

Secondly, God's children are to demonstrate all of His

characteristics and attributes. One of those attributes is to judge. He commands Aaron in Leviticus 10:10, "And that ye may put a difference between holy and unholy and between unclean and clean." Morally, this commandment yet stands. If God deems a sexual act or anything else as unclean, we are bound to stand with His judgment.

Finally, Jesus himself gave us the proper guidelines to judge. He revealed in John 7:24 that his followers were to judge. *Not according to appearance, but with righteous judgment.* How does one judge righteous judgment? Because all of us are still subject to potentially sin, we must all follow one uniform standard of judgment, which is God's Word. I'm no more qualified to tell you what is right than you are qualified to tell me what is right or wrong. Hence, we have God's Word. That's righteous judgment.

Jesus told us to make sure we get the mote out of our own eye, before we try to take the beam out of our brother's eye. For those who fail to live by this law of temperance and love, they will soon fall to the sins that lie in wait at their own doors.

But also, as I have passionately called for in this book, there must be a balance. While we cannot look at those who have sinned and suffered behind it with disdain or superiority, their lives of failure must serve as an example to those who live as they do. If we ignore the hurt, pain, failure and great loss, then we are doomed to repeat their failures. Paul wrote in 1 Corinthians 10:11,12:

> *Now all these things happened unto them for ensample [examples] and they are written for our admonition [warning], upon whom the ends of the world are come. Wherefore, let him that thinketh he standeth, take heed, lest he fall.*

The "things" Paul spoke of were Isreal's sins against God in the wilderness. He also warned the church of "ignorance" of the result of these sins. I talked about the terrible wrong I engaged in with as much honesty as I could, for several reasons. The most important being my hope that those who see what unfolded in my life will turn and avoid the same pitfalls. That must be the reason God let me live through all of the mess I walked in. "Tell them", Andrae Crouch plaintively sang once, "even if they don't believe you, just tell them, even if they don't receive you."

The men I chose to profile in this last part were examples also. They were men of immense talents and tremendous contributions; at times soaring in popularity and influence in their lifestyle circles. But, they have been silenced. Sin, the hit man from hell, tracked them down and assassinated them in cold blood. Others have told their stories from differing points of view, but here other facts and observations have been compiled to present a picture which, convincingly shouts to anyone with an ear to hear "watch out, reality kills!"

My purpose is not to paint them as freaks or losers, nor to disparage their humanity and personhood. I don't know why God allows some to sin and experience tragic results, and others sin, but turn to Him and find restoration.

Each of the men profiled should have served as an example to the church of today. There are so many important lessons we still can learn, if we lay aside our ignorance and ask God to give us wisdom to deal with homosexuality in our midst. If we choose to puff up and get angry (like some of the Corinthians did with Paul, 1 Corinthians 5:2), then we are set and will continue to experience the full force of devastation that homosexual sin, is wreaking on God's church.

BLACK OUT: BISHOP JOHN DELL HUSBAND

Back in the old days, homosexuality was whispered about, but rarely spoken of openly. Case in point, the murky story of one of my former denomination's most prolific preachers, the late Bishop John D. Husband. A resident of Atlanta, he presided over one the Church of God in Christ's rising jurisdictions, Central Georgia.

Bishop Husband was consecrated during a time of great turmoil in the church and eventually elected to the church's highest governing body, the General Board. Hushed up homosexual scandals were not just relegated to the pews, but the leadership was beset with them also. The church held its collective breath in early 1991, when a scandal of epic proportions surfaced involving the bishop.

"He [Husband] seemed like a very fine person. He was involved, as I remember, in some scandalous situation. Apparently, he did not survive the reaction; so they must have put him down.", said a former Missions Department COGIC Bishop who asked not to be named.

The *Atlanta Journal Constitution*[23,24] as well as Memphis' *Commercial Appeal*[25] reported in several successive articles that Bishop Husband had been accused of embezzling over half a million dollars of church money. Although the sex scandals were public knowledge, AJC reporters agreed not to print the initial stories of Husband's homosexuality because of the young boys and men involved.

As one of the original members of the church's presidium, he was held in great esteem by some, but secretly despised by others. According to one Texas church "superintendent", Bishop Husband's homosexuality was no secret in the denomination. Yet, year after year he was a favorite speaker at the national Holy Convocation in Memphis, a polished and dynamic personality who could move the

COGIC faithful with his preaching. But why church leadership never dealt with his mounting homosexual displays is still a mystery. Or if he was disciplined, why was it ineffective?

Rumors about Husband's increasingly open sexual proclivities began swirling madly like Texas tornadoes until the deafening roars reached the wary ears of Memphis 600 miles to the west. Even in Memphis, during church meetings, some that encountered him say his words and actions were very questionable.

A Pastor (who has since left the denomination) recalled a meeting with Husband: "Once in Memphis, I was with some friends at a restaurant and we happened to bump in to him at about 2 AM. He was always the only General Board member who hung out all hours of the night at the meetings, and now I know why. Anyway, he made a disparaging remark about [my Bishop]. I quickly defended [my Bishop] and let Bishop Husband know that I did not think that a Bishop would disrespect another Bishop like that. He gave a weak apology and offered to make it up later on if I called his hotel room. Needless to say, I never called and I never had a personal encounter with him. I have no idea how he was going to make it up, and I didn't want to find out."[26]

Husband's own wife Joann, who divorced him in the late seventies, is said to have reported him numerous times to the General Board in Memphis, complaining of his homosexual adultery and liaisons, but to no avail. The top presbytery refused to act, possibly because they were the ones who appointed him in 1965. The failure of the board to act swiftly and decisively with their contemporary may have pushed him to even further into the double lifestyle.

What happens when a church goes to war?

201

Husband was no novice. He was voted in as one of the original General Board members of the church, a consequence of the intense infighting in the church after the death of it's founder, C.H. Mason in 1961. Due to the internal conflicts sweeping across the church, Husband was one of 6 men appointed to Bishop. The behind the scenes struggles for loyalty may have pushed the church's "Executive Board" to attempt a counteraction of Bishop Ozro T. Jones Sr. appointments.

What happens when a church goes to war — against itself? On February 3, 1965, a meeting was convened at Pentecostal Temple in Memphis by the Executive Board to address the problem of church authority. At the center of the controversy was Bishop OT Jones, Sr.

The Executive Board[27], a small group of 11 Bishops contended in a letter, that although OT Jones had been "recognized and honored" as Senior Bishop in 1962, the agreement was that his office "would be worked out in April, 1963."[28] Apparently, Jones did not see things that way. The EB went on to say that "Bishop Jones, has since 1962, usurped the power of the Executive Board and abrogated unto himself the authority to appoint Bishops, Overseers and other officials of the church." Clearly, this was an angry group of men. They officially ordered Jones to "cease and desist."[29]

Later that year, October 6, another larger group, the Board of Bishops, asserted it's muscle on Jones' behalf. They also convened in Memphis and issued a stinging document asserting that they, not the Executive Board, had the power and that they affirmed the authority of Bishop Jones in the church.

The Board of Bishops strongly rebuked the EB, telling them that they would not recognize any "unauthorized acts, documents, credentials, decisions, appointments, meetings, financial obligations, agreements, "new" jurisdictions, and the like."[30]

Tucked within that rebuke was Bishop Husband's earlier appointment. Both powerful groups claimed that they were acting on the express authority of the deceased Bishop Mason.

The conflict remained unresolved and escalated to frightening heights. On January 23, 1968, a weary OT Jones himself issued a church-wide letter again spelling out the conditions of his authority. Like Paul defending his apostolic authority to the Corinthians, Jones pointed out that he was the last of the first five Bishops appointed by CH Mason. He said that Mason specifically chose him to hold the current office and "edit and codify and arrange the Church's Constitution, Doctrines, and rules of Order."

Jones lengthy letter issued several challenges to his opponents, pointing out that every time he was brought to court, it had been either resolved or thrown out. The matter was resolved, though not to everyone's satisfaction, by the formation of the General Board in 1969, with Bishop JO Patterson, Sr. being elected as the first "Presiding Bishop."

Personal and Painful

Although Husband (a favorite of J.O. Patterson, Sr.) later became one of the oratorical stars of the church, he skipped serious scrutiny of his personal life. That is, until the problems with money began.

One source stated that the embezzled money was a direct result of the homosexuality. It was strongly believed the money was used to pay for the medical bills of the male lover who passed the HIV virus on to the Bishop. A member of his local church, Elder Willie Davis and a plaintiff in the lawsuit against the Bishop, told the *Journal Constitution* "I don't know that if he's used this money for his personal benefit, but it's gone somewhere."

The Atlanta saga was becoming more and more disturbing while Husband spun a wider web of sexual involvement with young men mostly within his jurisdiction.

Gwen Fox, now getting up in age, knew firsthand the anguish of Husband's sexual outreaches. Her son "Toby" (Tobias) ~whose birthday was the same as Husband~ was molested by the bishop during the church's Memphis meeting in 1981.[31] The anguish behind years of dealing with the situation caused her to suffer 3 heart attacks and other personal losses including estrangement from the church she loved so much.

Toby, 15 or 16 at the time, was overjoyed that his mom had allowed him to accompany Bishop Husband to the meeting. Husband was given money to pay for a separate room for the boy, but when they both arrived in Memphis, Husband lied to the boy telling him that there were no rooms available. Further, he said that the two of them would have to share a room. Toby was now in the molester's grip. He recalled that the Bishop's subtle sexual advances began much earlier than 13.

Husband's predatory activities against young boys began long before he was appointed to Bishop. He was brought to Atlanta from Mississippi as a protege of the late Bishop James Hinsley. A one time mail carrier, Husband lived with the Hinsley family for some time. But trouble surfaced when neighbors complained to police that Husband was enticing and molesting young boys. A trap door in the back of the store he owned served as the portal to those unspeakable acts. Gwen Fox recalls that the late Bishop W.G. Shipman came to town and quietly bailed Husband out of jail after two arrests. In Memphis, Toby was trapped and cornered.

"When Toby returned home, his behavior begin to change. He started having trouble at school and it got so bad that the teachers begin to call me and ask if something bad was going on at home," she remembered.

Toby, twenty one years later and now stricken with HIV remembered that Husband had gotten in bed with him and begin forcefully pressing his genitals against the young boy. Shocked and bewildered, he jumped out of bed and asked Husband what he was doing.

He said Husband looked at him with a calm face and said, "I thought this was what you wanted." Tobias admitted that, at a later time, he willingly continued in a sexual relationship with Husband until his young adult years.

"He was powerful and I wanted to be connected to that. I (eventually) felt comfortable around him and wanted his love. He gave me the attention I needed, that I wanted from a man. He always told me 'you're the best, you're the best'", said the talented songwriter and musician.[32]

When Toby finally confessed to an aunt what had transpired in Memphis, Gwen Fox was told. She immediately began petitioning the church's General Board on behalf of her son. She said she sent certified letters to each member and even hand delivered a letter to then presiding Bishop Louis H. Ford, who angrily refused to accept it even after Fox had waited hours in line to see him.

Fox, whose parents were well known COGIC pioneers in Georgia, got angry herself and threatened to begin contacting talk shows — notably Oprah Winfrey — if the church leaders would not hear her. In retaliation, several anonymous death threats were made against her life.

She vividly recalled the night at Husband's Marietta church when several bishops from the church were there to investigate allegations of the financial improprieties. Because of the death threats and rumors of gun toting "saints", undercover police were sprinkled throughout the building.

"It was one terrible, terrible night," she said softly.

The meeting was coming to an end and not one Bishop had addressed the sexual allegations which affected so many. Refusing to be put off any longer, Fox and another woman whose son was a victim stood up and asked when they (the Bishops) were going to deal with Husband's sexual problems. Although she was initially rebuffed, Fox was later told to come back into the church offices to relate her story to the quorum of Bishops and officials.

"Some of them were mean and arrogant, others listened. Bishop O.T. Jones, Jr. cried when I told them my story. The President of the Marietta NAACP went with me because of the death threats that I had heard about. They even advised me to bring legal action against COGIC, but I didn't want to go against what the scriptures said." Another Bishop, believing the church to be liable for Husband's actions, also urged her to pursue litigation against the church.

At a special meeting in Memphis in early 1991, Husband, through his attorney, submitted a formal letter admitting guilt to "all charges." He was summarily stripped of all credentials and excommunicated from the church, the first time COGIC had done so with any Bishop. Yet, another California Bishop, who had served as the church's General Secretary, was left unscathed, even after Husband had allegedly named him as a sexual partner on a medical document.

Possibly sick of disease, Husband died in late 1991 of unpublicized causes. COGIC erased what part of his legacy and contributions to the church they could. His funeral, held at Rev. Timothy Fleming's Mt. Carmel Baptist Church in Atlanta, was not attended by any of the COGIC General Board.

A sad and disturbing chapter in the church that could have been used positively to deal with future problems were simply swept under the rug. Some say this was done for several reasons. One, besides the General Secretary, there were at least two other national officers who were following in Husband's path. They felt more scandals could severely damage the already tarnished reputation of a church reeling from years of infighting. Secondly, perhaps the most tragic, blacking out Husband's transgressions helped to ease the guilt on their souls.

THE KING COMETH: REV. JAMES CLEVELAND

In the late 70s and 80s, Black gospel music began a remarkable renaissance march towards national recognition among other musical genres. But along with the emergence of the music, with its spirited sound and the energetic performances of choirs, groups and soloists, a dark side snaked alongside it, gaining ground with each new album and each new concert. One of the most infamous scandals to rock the black gospel music world was the breaking news of the longtime involvement of its self-appointed "king" the Rev. James Cleveland, with homosexuality.

Al Hobbs, a past Chairman of the Gospel Announcers Guild called Cleveland a "musical genius" whose works " have been the standard by which an entire musical genre has been measured."[33]

Cleveland's brusque voice was a developing force in gospel music for decades. His venerable influence on countless artists is irrefutable, but after his own AIDS-related death February 9, 1991 at age 59, young men who had allegedly been infected with the virus by Cleveland came forth with damning accusations of Cleveland's penchant for young boys. Young boys he enticed, manipulated and sexually used in the course of his "reign" as the king of gospel music.

Demand for James Cleveland's musical prowess was insatiable. He wrote more than 400 songs and church anthems, recorded 100 albums (16 of them went gold) and won 4 Grammys. Songs like "I don't feel noways tired", "To Jesus I'll Go", "Jesus Saves" and "God has smiled on me" are considered black church classics. His crowning achievement was the founding of the Gospel Music Workshop of America (GMWA) the largest independent gospel convention of it's kind. Over the years, the GMWA gained a reputation for fostering a behind the scenes atmosphere of debauchery and promiscuity.

A music ministry insider said that the information on Rev Cleveland and the GMWA is only partially true. After viewing the GMWA website he had this to say:

"What's not listed is the whoredom and rampant sin from the executive board on down. The bio on Cleveland makes him appear to be a role model. In reality, he was a whore who ruined a lot of lives in the name of gospel music. His nickname in the 70's was La Founder. Even though the GMWA gave a lot of opportunities for up and coming artists and there was a facade of Christianity, the truth is that it was a big party. It's a shame that Youth Choir leaders could not let their choir members walk the halls of the hotels alone for fear of being approached by older men and women."

"Some of the wild parties and orgies given by choirs, including Cleveland's Southern California Community Choir, caused security to evict them from the hotel. Yes, there were people trying to live right, but the leadership set the tone for the convention and it was not a good one. I think reality is that we don't want to believe that it is happening in the upper levels of most churches."

He continued, "At one of the conventions, James invited me and a couple of the other tenors to a cookout at his house in LA and our director emphatically say NO and yelled at him for inviting us. We thought she was being overly protective but thank God for the protection. Some times I shudder to think that I was so close to harm, and yet God protected me and I'm sure others."

James Cleveland, like many others living the fragmented life of homosexuality, became seductive trees of good and evil. For all of his immense talent and influence on the world of gospel music, he stamped a dark legacy of homosexuality that has haunted the music world since that time.

Eclectic online spiritual scribe Christopher J. Priest of DigitalPriest.com echoed widespread beliefs about Cleveland's terrible legacy.

"Cleveland was, as reported to me by musicians who played with him, a ruthless exploiter of the race and the Gospel, a friend to few, and a deeply conflicted and troubled individual. His annual Gospel Music Workshop of America, which continues and thrives to this day, is, to my thinking, one of the worst examples of Christianity, as it thrives on competitiveness and ruthless exploitation of young talent, as well as being a Gomorrahish annual Drag Queen fest (it was commonly accepted that Cleveland was gay; a lifestyle the black church largely turned a blind eye to. To this day, the black church turns a blind eye to matters of infidelity and sexual orientation as suits its purpose while paradoxically condemning both as it sees fit; love and understanding doled out based on social position)."[34]

Though I had loved and sung his songs many times before, I was completely unaware of the strong undercurrent of homosexuality in Cleveland's life and in the gospel music world. James, a close gay military friend of mine from Newport News, Virginia shocked me with his eyewitness accounts of the infamous rehearsals at the GMWA conventions. He said he attended several years in a row until he lost interest in it.

"Darryl, that place [convention] is like a Roman orgy!", he exclaimed. James, through slightly crossed eyes, peered at me, surprised that I didn't know or hadn't heard. "James Cleveland was always after those boys and inviting them back to his room." After his death, some of those boys began to talk.

One of those young men who came forward was Christopher Harris of Los Angeles. Harris, who once called himself Christopher Cleveland told a reporter [James] Cleveland exercised so much emotional and mental control over him, he felt owned.

"Legally, I became his." he said. Harris said his 5-year long sexual encounters with the larger than life gospel icon began when he was 13 and the only male alto in Cleveland's Cornerstone Baptist Church choir. Harris admitted Cleveland was not his first male sexual encounter nor did he consider the relationship "molestation." But he knew that his sexual relationship with Cleveland was a lopsided match in which Cleveland exploited relentlessly.

He told the Wilmington Delaware *Sunday News Journal*[35], "I went to his church. He looked into my face and saw my dreams and he used it. I wanted to sing. I didn't want to be like him. He promised that he would help me. He just played it to his advantage, he used my naivetes to his advantage."

Since that time literally thousands of older "mentors" and young men have followed in Cleveland and Harris' adjective steps, living out the terrible roles of perpetrator and victim, while singing in the gospel music tradition of "lifting up the name of Jesus in song." How ironic that the Jesus they sang of seemed never to convict their hearts about the destructive behavior they practiced outside of the choir lofts.

Donnie McClurkin echoed the secret sexual underworld of the church, further proof that the Clevelandesque predators still seek the young and the vunerable.

"I discovered that there were VULTURES, also in the church (predatory men that would soon attempt to take advantage of a broken boy and his confusion.) I discovered that in the homosexual lifestyle, when you're young, you are the prey to be hunted. But when you get older, and lose youthfulness, you become the predator.", he said.[36]

Popular host of "Bobby Jones Gospel", Bobby Jones speculated to the *News Journal* that James Cleveland's career might have been ruined if it was found out that he had AIDS [from homosexual relationships]. Christopher Harris said that Cleveland's "secret" lifestyle of male sexual encounters were "typical" of the many people in the industry he was exposed to.

PROFILE 3 - A SHOOTING STAR: SYLVESTER

Nobody wanted this party to stop! It was a sweltering summer night in Richmond, Virginia and the gay club Scandals International was cranking up the dance floor speakers and letting the liquor run free.

Jennifer Beals and her "flashdance" look had turned the fashion world on its head. Long lines of men wore slashed jeans and shirts, revealing a hint of exhibitionism. The crowds itching to get inside worshipped it as the style coup of the moment. Inside, the DJs were already pumping and priming the capacity crowds for the night's main attraction. The San Francisco disco superstar, Sylvester was getting ready to make everyone feel mighty real.

The $15 cover charge was steep, but well worth it for the chance to see Sylvester's maximum impact performance. Sylvester's twin mega hits "Dance (Disco Heat)" and "You make me feel (mighty real)" stood like the pre911 World Trade Center towers of the disco world.

Sylvester's incomparable voice -- soaring, diving, rippling and screaming over the galloping disco beats -- was like a vocal circus. It pushed partygoers right over the edge. Sylvester's singing almost made you feel like you were back in church, with his strong gospel-sounding vocal arrangements. His punctuated notes invited you to shout and dance right along with him. He was having a good time and his music transformed the homeliest of club wallflowers into wildflowers.

A spiritual experience? Some insist it was. Only this was not about the Lord. And it wasn't about singing His praises.

That night I, along with hundreds of others waited breathlessly in the "grand ballroom" for the show to begin. I was a little curious, a little nervous but determined to accept and enjoy what I discovered as part of my new, enunciated interest in the gay life.

At 11 pm sharp, he appeared. An audible gasp escaped from the crowd. Then suddenly, as he lifted his hands, total silence fell upon the the crowd as if in the presence of royalty. I too, was stunned.

Adorned in a shimmering gold costume from head to toe, he launched into his passionate remake of Freda Payne's old classic, Band of Gold. Sylvester was simply put, a star. He possessed an uncanny ability to *be* what he was actually singing. It was a talent few had.

But though a book appears to be exciting, the pages telling it's story can be altogether different. So it was with Sylvester, gay Richmond's "goddess-for-a-night". Behind the well-oiled glitter and the glamorous female persona mask was a young man who was deeply troubled. And deeply scarred from a childhood sexual violation.

Born Sylvester James in either 1944 or 1946 from some reports in Los Angeles, he was raised and taught to sing by his grandmother, blues singer Julia Morgan. Apparently, his first love was the church. His first big hit, "Mighty Real" was actually written as a gospel tune.[37]

Although it's unclear exactly which church he attended, in 1980 he revealed that he was molested at age seven by a church evangelist. The interview was done by Adam Block writing for *The Advocate*, a gay newsmagazine. Years later, still emotionally simmering over the hypocrisy of the church, he bitterly told a friend, "The same ones who turned me out, put me out [of the church]."

His feminine identity surfaced early in his life, beginning a lifelong obsession with transvestism, even dressing as a woman for the last three years of high school. A tell-tell sign of his ambitions was his senior photo, in which he posed with a string of pearls over his graduating gown. Sylvester's natural ability at theatrics soon caught the attention of record producers who began writing and producing songs that would secure him a massive following among San Francisco's homosexual population.

The powerful falsetto voice, which was reported to range eight octaves, was the driving force behind the songs he sang. Sylvester took the sound of gospel music and married it to the emerging frenetic beats of disco/dance and in the process made himself a star. Most of his songs were, at closer examination, about love desired, but never attained. The themes centered on partying or longing for someone to to love, the two extremes of gay life. Along the way, Sylvester received the accolades of many who met him --and worked with him on mutual projects-- among them Aretha Franklin, Patty Labelle and Gladys Knight, Cher, Daryl Coley and Lynette Hawkins-Stephens.

Sylvester was never at a loss for words or one to dress "normal" when performing. His wildly outrageous costumes became his trademark alongside his unique voice. But interesting enough, though he was the toast of the gay community and immersed himself in its culture, he never seemed to completely lose his attraction to the church and its influence on him.

He lost his life to AIDS in 1988, and was buried in full drag (women's clothing) at Love Center Church and eulogized by now Bishop Walter Hawkins.[38] Hawkins' website bio, acknowledges he has "collaborated with a number of artists". But here Sylvester, the openly gay man who lived much of his life as a feminine persona was only mentioned as "the late House Music King."[39]

THE FINAL PERFORMANCE - RAYMOND A. MYLES

New Orleans, the Crescent City was home to many outstanding Gospel music stars, among them the famed matriarch Mahalia Jackson. The city of diverse eccentrics such as Mardi Gras and cajun food was also home for another Gospel star named Raymond Anthony Myles.

A product of the St Bernard housing projects, Myles was an incredible performer who at the tender age of 12 sang at Mahalia's funeral. From that point on, it was clear that Myles would become a powerfully profiled entertainer on the local music scene. When Myles showed up to do a concert, attendees were guaranteed to get their money's worth and much more. Raymond was the consummate performer. He knew what the people liked and wanted and he delivered it to them with seeming effortless unction. His musical orations kept them coming back, hungry for more and more.

A reviewer of one of his gospel releases, "A Taste of Heaven", described Myles thusly: "Raymond Myles is a gospel singer with show-stopping, hair-raising talent. Raymond has been compared to Little Richard in personality, Stevie Wonder in range and power, Donnie Hathaway in spirit and Micheal Jackson in moves."[40]

But behind the man and his musical charisma was a dangerous weakness, that in the end, not even his own honey-dripped voice could save him from.

"I knew Raymond Myles and his mother [Christine] personally for many years. He was openly gay and very feminine.", said a former resident of New Orleans.[41]

Myles' homosexuality and affinity for the feminine began showing up early in his musical foray. Acquaintances say that he wore foundational makeup and women's furs in the early seventies but later developed a "gay thug" persona. Christine Myles herself seemed disturbed by her son's changing personality.

The former resident remembers, "Ms Chris" as she was called by those who knew her, "was singing on a program and Raymond, (who was around 17 or 18 at the time) was backing her up on the organ. While she was talking, she said 'pray for my son, I borned [sic] him a boy, but I don't know what he is now'." It appears very few people, if any, wanted to stand in the way of Myles's march to success. Though he was hailed as gospel singer he tried very hard to be anything but a gospel singer. As he grew more successful, some say his makeup and clothing grew more outlandish.

Neither did Raymond's obvious flamboyance and homosexuality, prevent him from moving comfortably in the church circles of New Orleans. He served intermittently as organist at Greater St Stephen's Full Gospel Baptist Church under Bishop Paul Morton, Sr., but primarily plied his craft at Greater Asia Baptist Church under the late Rev. Zebedee Bridges. It was reported that Raymond's organ prowess sounded like a "12 piece R&B horn section." If anyone seemed to have it all , it was Raymond Myles. A chorus of secular and gospel voices praised him and his gift untiringly.

Billboard Magazine wrote adoringly of him in its June 14, 1997 issue, calling him "New Orleans best kept secret and decreed he was "poised for major leap into the mainstream." The lights, camera and action of big time gospel performing was a stark contrast to the private Raymond. He began cruising the streets of New Orleans and picking up "street trade" for sex. Eventually, this practice would end in his final performance.

Gospel fans of Myles pointedly overlooked his disdain for the very gospel music he sang. In public interviews, he attempted to distance himself from it as much as possible. Frequently, he so blurred the lines between the secular and the sacred it was impossible to know whether the Holy Spirit or human hype was driving his intense performances.

In an interview with NYNO Records, Myles was asked what were the five favorite records in his personal collection. He listed all secular artists and himself. He stated his favorite song was the R&B crossover, "I believe I can fly, by R. Kelly. Those comments agree with what others in New Orleans remember about him.

"My problem with this whole Raymond Myles gospel singer thing is if he was such a lover of gospel, why is that all of his favorites were secular songs, hangouts and artists?", questioned one detractor. "It's sad, Raymond was talented, but far from spiritual."[42]

The defiance of, and longing for the acceptance of the church fueled Myles' pressing desire to act independently of what people wanted him to be. He believed he was bigger than the church, but his roots held him to it in a way that both infuriated him and soothed him.

At the age of 12, he shocked and embarrassed his mother by recording the song "You made a man out of me, baby." The recording immediately gained him 2 things: secular recognition and church scorn.

The defiance of, and perhaps longing for the acceptance of the church, fueled Myles' pressing desire to act independently of what people wanted him to be. He believed he was bigger than the church, but his roots held him to it in a way that both infuriated him and soothed him. At the age of 12, he shocked and embarrassed his mother by recording the song "You made a man out of me, baby." The recording immediately gained him 2 things: secular recognition and church scorn.

He told writer Jonathan Tabak in a 1996 interview, "I wanted to be me. And I had a problem with people accepting me, okay, and when I found out who I was, and when I found out *whose* I was, life became better for me. I was never a religious person. I was reared in the church because that's all I knew...I don't want to be known as being a gospel singer. I am an entertainer."[43] Myles had planned to do an album of secular love songs and R&B "message" music, but it never materialized.[44]

Raymond continued racking up accolade after accolade and praise after praise, but time was winding up for the star. Around the corner lurked a violent death, the consequence of his lust for the type of men he grew up around back in St. Bernard's.

On the night of October 11, 1998, Myles was cruising around the city in his white Lincoln Navigator looking for his usual sexual diet of down and out thugs. He found two of them. Later, the maestro Myles was discovered lying in the street, dead of gunshot wounds. The two men who killed him were quickly branded "carjackers" by the police. But those who knew of Myles' dangerous activities said the real surprise was that he had not been murdered sooner.

Resources

Books and Discipleship Manuals
The Billy Graham Christian Worker's Handbook
Billy Graham World Wide Publications, 1984, Minneapolis, MN

Counseling the Homosexual
Earl Wilson, Word Publishing, 1988, Dallas

Eternal Victim/Eternal Victor
Donnie McClurkin, Pnuema Life Publishing, 2001, Lanham, MD

How on Earth can I be Spritual?
C. Sumner Wemp, Thomas Nelson Publishers, 1978, Nashville

Getting a Grip on the Basics
Beth Jones, Harrison House, 1994,Tulsa

More Than You Know
DL Foster, Self published, 2001, Atlanta

Homosexuality: State of Birth or State of Mind?
Dr. Frederick K.C. Price, Faith One Publishing, Los Angeles

Holy Sex
Terry Wier w/Mark Carruth, Whitaker House, 1999, New Kensington, PA

An Ounce of Prevention
Don Schmierer, Word Publishing, 1998, Dallas

A Strong Delusion
Joe Dallas, Harvest House, 1996, Eugene, OR

A Way of Escape
Neil Anderson, Gospel Light Publishing

Eros Defiled
John White, Inter-Varsity Press, 1977, Downers Grove, IL

World Wide Web
WITNESS! Freedom Ministries, Inc.
www.witnessfortheworld.org

Exodus International, NA
www.exodusnorthamerica.org

Out of the Fire Ministries
www.miriamisout.org

Mighty Through God Ministry
www.mtg.faithweb.com

He Intends Victory (HIV/AIDS) Ministry
www.heintendsvictory.com

Beacon Ministries (for Apostolic overcomers)
www.beaconministries.homestead.com/index.html

Parents and Friends of Exgays (PFOX)
www.pfox.com

Deep Blue Fusion
www.deepbluefusion.com

Regeneration Books
www.exodusnorthamerica.org/resources

Endnotes

Chapter 2
[1]William B. McClain, "African American Preaching," *Leadership Handbook of Preaching and Worship* (Grand Rapids, MI, Baker Books, 1992) , 75-76

Chapter 3
[2] DL Foster, "Inner Healing or Delivering Power",*The Stone Tablet*,Sep 1999
[3]John W. Hole, Jr, "Blood", *Human Anatomy and Physiology Sixth Edition* (Dubuque, IA, Wm C. Brown Books, 1993) 6

Chapter 4
[4]Dr.Jim Hopper, "Sexual Abuse of Males: Prevalence, Possible Lasting Effects, and Resources", http://www.jimhopper.com/male-ab/, 6 Mar 2001

Chapter 5
[5]CDC Media Relations, "Suicide among black youths, 20 Mar 1998
[6] CDC unpublished mortality data from the National Center for Health Statistics (NCHS) Mortality Data Tapes.

Chapter 7

[7] Joe Dallas, "How it began (1950-1969)" *A Strong Delusion* (Eugene, OR Harvest House, 1996)

Chapter 8

[8] The Apostle Paul addressed both sexual positions in 1 Corinthians 6:9-11. Though pro-gay Bible revisionists have staunchly argued that Paul had no concept of "loving, monogamous gay relationships," they nevertheless have performed interpretive magic tricks to form fit the scripture to their opinions.

Chapter 15

[9] Text James Rowe, 1865-1933; tune SAFETY, 7 6 7 6 7 6 7 4 with refrain, Howard E. Smith, 1863-1918

[10] Mark Tooley, "Ecumenical student conference includes pro gay themes" Institute on Religion and Democracy, 4 Jan 1999,http://www.ucmpage.org/umaction/mtooley14. htm, 6 Jan 2002

Chapter 18

[11] Matthew James, Jr, Who's Leading the Choir?: Homosexuality in the Black Church

[12] Spiros Zodhiates, *The Hebrew-Greek Keyword Study Bible*, 1991, AMG Publishers, Chattanooga. The word **perfect** in Ephesians 4:13 is from the Greek "telelos", meaning goal or purpose. It portrays an image of fully completed growth, as contrasted with infancy and childhood. Compare with "anamartesia", used to ascribe perfection to God. The latter denotes unblemished sinlessness, without efforts to attain it.

Chapter 20

[13] Donnie McClurkin, "The Fight is On", *Eternal Victim/Eternal Victor*, (Lanham, MD, Pneuma Life Publishing, 2001) 99

[14] Dr. Frederick K.C. Price, "What the Church has Allowed", *Race, Religion & Racism, Volume 1* (Los Angeles, Faith One Publishing,1999)16

[15] Dr. Frederick K.C. Price, "The White Distortion", *Race, Religion &Racism, Volume 2* (Los Angeles,Faith One Publishing, 1999)4

[16] Some black ministers openly welcoming gays, lesbians, MSNBC, http://www. msnbc.com/local/rtga/m183948.asp?cp=1=1, 17 May 2002

[17] Jeremiah Wright, excerpt from the sermon entitled "Good News for the homosexual."*The Spiritual Perspective*, Chicago, May 1999, ppgs 6,7 "I have been the ministerial outcast among many of my colleagues for some fifteen years because I refuse to believe that my God loves only some of his world. My Bible does not say,

"For God so loved some of the world—or most of the world—that he gave his only begotten Son that any heterosexual who believes in him. My Bible says all the world and whosoever—not those I like. Whosoever—not those who are like me. Whosoever. I refuse to limit my God, to lock God into my cultural understandings because culture is fickle. And culture is often wrong. Culture was wrong about slavery. Culture was wrong about women. Culture was wrong about Africans and Indians, and culture was wrong about Christ. I refuse to limit my God, to lock God into little cultural prisons, no matter how comfortable those prisons may feel. I refuse to leave my brain at the door when I come into God's presence to worship or when I read God's Word. And because I refuse, I have been the pariah among many of my clergy colleagues who somehow see me as defective or not quite saved because I won't join them in their homophobic gay bashing and misquoting of Scripture."

[18] Andrew Craig, http://www.narrowgate.net/~bsnider/birthofpentecost.html, 16 Aug 2001

[19] Genesis 1:27, Gen 6:19, Gen 9:20-24, Gen 10:15-19, Gen19:4-9, Leviticus 5:3 Lev 18:22,30; Lev 20:13, Deuteronomy 22:5, Deut 23:17, Judges 2:11-13 Judges 19:22-24, 1 Kings 14:22-24, 1 Kings 15:11-12, Ezekiel 16:49, Daniel 11:37, Romans 1:18-28, Gal 5:19,Eph 5:3-7, Col 3:5-7, 1 Tim1:10, Titus 1:15-16, Jude 4,7,19;
1Corinthians 6:9-11, Rev 21:27

[20] From a sermon delivered at Living Word Cogic, Waco, TX

[21] From a radio broadcast of (former) Wynnton Rd Cogic on WOKS-AM, Columbus, GA

[22] From a sermon preached at Ephesians Cogic, Berkley,CA

Appendix

Bishop JD Husband

[23] Gayle White, "Bishop faces inquiry: Church of God in Christ looks for missing funds" *Atlanta Journal and Constitution*, 28 Jan 1991, D/01

[24] Gayle White, "Pentecostal Group on a Roll", *Atlanta Journal and Constitution*, 6 Apr 1991, E/06

[25] Tom Bailey, Jr., "COGIC Probes Loan, Replaces GA Bishop", *The Commercial Appeal*,5 Feb 1991,B1

[26] Unnamed Source, Personal electronic Interview, 11Nov 2001

[27]The Executive Board members present at this meeting consisted of Bishops A.B

McEwen, J.S. Bailey, W.G. Shipman,Wyoming Wells, J.O.Patterson, Sr.,C.E. Bennett, B.S.Lyle, John White, S.M. Crouch, E.E. Hamilton, and C.H. Brewer.

[28] Elder EF Foster, personal correspondence, letter addressed to COGIC clergy from the Executive Board, Memphis, Feb 1965

[29] ibid

[30] The Official Message of the Board of Bishops of the COGIC, Norfolk, VA, 6 Oct, 1965

[31] Personal interview with Gwendolyn Fox, Atlanta, 20 Feb 2002

[32] Personal interview with Tobias Fox, Atlanta 9 May 2002

Rev James Cleveland

[33] Rhonda Graham, "And the Choir sings On," The Wilmington Delaware Sunday News-Journal, 23 Oct 1994

[34] Al Hobbs, CD Project Commentary, "A Tribute to James Cleveland", A&M Records, 1991

[35] A time to dance: Kim Burrell and the Black Church's obsession with 1965, http://www.Digital-Priest.com, 2 Feb 2002

Sylvester

[36] Alan X, "Sex,Drugs and Sylvester", http://www.shf.at, 21 Nov 2001

[37] Funeral program for Sylvester James, 19 Dec 1988

[38] Walter Hawkins Biography, 26 Dec 2001, http://www.lovecenter.org/Whawkinsbio.htm

Raymond Myles

[39] Jonathan Tabak, Raymond Anthony Myles, 11 Nov 2001, http://www.offbeat.com/text/rev6.html

[40] Source unnamed by request, personal electronic interview, 14 Nov 2001

[41] Ibid

[42] NNYO Records, Raymond Myles: Bio FAQs, http://www.nynorecords.com/raymond.shtml, 10 Nov 2001

[43] Jonathan Tabak, "Fest focus: Raymond Myles", http://www.offbeat.com/text/myles.html, 11 Nov 2001